# HEARTFUL

Embracing the courageous journey
to live a fulfilling heart-led life
through the power of connection

Essi Auguste Virtanen

Book Cover Design by Lauren Andrews, Simply Good Studio
Book edited by Merlina San Nicolás Leyva
1st edition – 2023

# DEDICATION

This book is dedicated to my family; mom, dad, and brother Elias who have always allowed me to follow my heart, even when it might have not made sense to them and meant we have had a lot of time apart living in different countries.

Thank you for accepting me and loving me for who I am.

I love you.

And to my brother Esa, who we lost way too soon.

You are the reason I keep connecting and moving and want to help others to do the same.

This book would not be, if it weren't for you.

*"Remember that wherever your heart is, there you will also find your treasure."*

— **Paulo Coelho, *The Alchemist***

# TABLE OF CONTENTS

# PROLOGUE

*"Don't let the noise of others' opinions drown out your inner voice. And most important, have the courage to follow your heart and intuition."*

— **Steve Jobs**

When I first found out about the word heartfulness, I was living in East London doing my Master's degree and trying to figure out my thesis subject. I was browsing online going through different subjects of positive psychology and wondering what interested me the most.

Then the word found me: *Heartfulness.* I subsequently found about the Heartfulness Meditation movement that defines heartfulness as *"an ideal, a spiritual way of living by and from the heart that is inclusive of all ideologies, beliefs, and religions."*

I soon found out that in positive psychology literature *heartfulness* had not been discussed much beyond the Heartfulness Meditation, and I became determined to look into where heartfulness came from, what it really was about, and explore how people experience it.

As I embarked on writing my thesis study on this subject, I found the definition that this book and philosophy is based on. To capture a part of my thesis study:

*"The meaning of heartfulness is embodied in the kanji character 念, that entails two parts: 今, now; and 心, heart, which portrays the connection to the present moment awareness of mindfulness (Murphy-Shigematsu, 2018). In Japanese, the word shinzou is used for the physical organ of the heart but kokoro is a word of a more complex meaning.*

*"Kokoro unites feeling, emotion, mind, and spirit — the whole person — and seems close to the word heartfulness" (Murphy-Shigematsu, 2018, p. 16).*

*These semantic meanings present the contrast how in Western languages mind and heart are often expressed as separate. However, in the Eastern world heart and mind are often seen to describe "the whole person" as "one" and "the center," which sets the stage for mindfulness and heartfulness interconnectedness."*

**Heartfulness means living from your heart, being your whole self in united oneness and interconnectedness in self, others, the world, and something higher. Heartfulness is embodied courage of listening and actioning on your intuition - also called as the "callings of your heart."**

In retrospect, three years later writing this, little did I know that in that moment I had found something that I had practiced and lived by my entire life, but I just did not have the word to call it so. Little did I know that a few years later I would write a book about it.

So, here we are.

**TRAVELING THE ROAD LESS TRAVELED**

My entire life, I have been driven by the courage of my heart. To travel the road less traveled and create a life on my own terms. To follow my heart's callings, even if it was incredibly scary.

Whether it was me at 16, wanting to use all of my savings for an English language course in London to go live in the city and practice my English that at the time was very broken still, or moving to Oxford to work in a hotel and practice further a few years later.

In 2014, I took the biggest leap yet as I jumped on a plane across the Atlantic, and left my family, friends, and everything I knew behind to study journalism in the US to perfect my English and written expression. My goal was to become the best communicator I can be in English so that one day people thought I was a native speaker.

The goal and destination were clear. To clarify, at this point, my English was still quite broken, and studying for a higher education degree was a big challenge in itself. I remember how much brain power it took me to get through reading for classes when sometimes I did not even know more than half the words. However, I knew in my heart that diving to the deep end like this was the way to fulfill my goal.

Three and a half years later, I graduated with the highest honors. I won awards in journalism. I wrote and workshopped a full-length play that I wrote. My first internship was with CNN in London.

It was around this time that I remember someone asking: *"Are you from the US? Your English is so good I would not have thought you were not native."*

**Goal accomplished.**

My heart was fulfilled and even to this day, writing this at the age of 30, every time someone points out my English-sounding native level - it just hits that spot all the same.


**STORYTELLING AS MY SAFEHAVEN AND DRIVER**

I always have had the drive to tell stories. Whether it was through poetry, short stories, or essays - I had been writing ever since I was young in secondary school. Therefore, journalism was a natural choice that I do not even remember choosing, it just felt right in my heart at the time. It was just this inner knowing for me that I wanted to make the world a better place through the vessel of storytelling.

This was because storytelling had made my world better.

It was Harry Potter and other fantasy books and writing my own fantasy short stories in secondary school that were my escape when I did not have that many friends and felt like an outsider. I had moved to the village a few years prior, and there was this sense of not belonging having been taken away from my childhood neighborhood and area.

J.K. Rowling's characters and mine were like friends to me. I know it sounds a bit silly, but it is the truth. When I felt lonely, I let my eyes wander on the pages of books or my pen to flow on the page for me to write my own - and I found belonging and friends there.

To this day I am deeply grateful for how stories helped me back then. From this experience, I knew the power of how the right story can make an impact, and this was the impact I was hoping to make going onward.

When I was writing and filming stories for my journalism degree, it was my driving force to share people's stories of resilience, inspiration, and drive for what fulfills their heart to inspire others to do the same. I mainly focused on writing features due to this, as I really wanted to get to the depth of a person and the story.

**A DEFINING MOMENT - FINDING MY DRIVING FORCE**

On April 19th, 2017, I faced the biggest loss of my life when my little brother died of suicide. The most bizarre thing is that a month prior I wrote a story about a Lacrosse player who died of suicide on our campus. I only realized it after, but I knew writing that story and interviewing his friends and coaches prepared my heart to face a loss of my own a month later.

**Stories have always been there to guide and support me.**

Losing my brother stands as a defining moment in my life to this day, and it opened my eyes to two things:

1.   Our wellbeing is our everything, and if we do not maintain or care for it, we got nothing.
2.   Secondly, telling stories for inspiration was not enough for me anymore, but I needed to find a way to help people to shape their own stories.

At this time in my last year of college, I had the privilege of being the editor-in-chief for our university publications. As my final issue as the editor, I decided I wanted us to create a magazine issue focused on mental health and wrote an investigative piece, *"Breaking the silence of mental health issues in college,"* for our university publication LindenLink.

For this story, I interviewed someone who had attempted suicide before, but who is thankfully still here. Sharing stories like hers to raise awareness was essential for me after the loss of my family, the Lacrosse team I had interviewed, and so many other people on this earth who had gone through the same before.

My driving force became: suicide has to stop, but just writing about it was not enough.

I wanted to be able to not just write about it. **I wanted to be able to guide people on their journey. To empower them that no matter what heartbreak or darkness they might face, they can see the light at the end of the tunnel and find their way back to it.**

My brother did not find his way back to the light; and to this day, he drives everything I do. **The heartbreak of his loss drives me to follow my heart to make a difference.**

**HEARTFULNESS: COURAGEOUS LIVING**

So, to go back to the moment during my Master's Degree, when I was reading more about heartfulness, something clicked. I realized I had lived heartfully, following my heart my entire life.

I have also come to learn that the most excruciating heartbreaks are our greatest teachers and guiding lights to our fulfillment. **The pain we go through makes us who we are meant to become.**

I would not be who I am without the pain I have gone through.

Additionally, heartful living is where you hear your heart's intuition and dare to act on its calling despite the fear it might spark within you.

**Heartfulness is courageous living.**

**It takes courage to live from your heart.**

It is very easy to remain in the mind and just live life in an automatic mode. However, if you let your heart step into the driver's seat, you are about to get a path where fulfillment can be found. If you dare to ask the fear to step into the backseat and allow your heart to drive with a clear mind, your body fully present, and your spirit empowered by your side in the shotgun seat - the whole of you is then driving your life.

**Everyone knows their roles and place to be, and you will find heartful harmony in your life.**

**I also call this holistic connection within you.**

A good example of this intuitive calling and following it was when after graduating from college in 2018, I was sitting at a café with a friend with whom we had graduated together, applying for jobs like good recent grads do. Then, out of the blue, it was as clear as a whisper that came from somewhere higher that I heard in my mind:

*"Go to LA."*

I had not thought about anything like that before. I took a moment to honor the whisper and jokingly said to my friend across the table.

*"Random idea, but what if we just got in the car and drove to LA and see what happens?"*

Three weeks later, we were in the car going with our degrees in our pockets, not much money, and no place to live; we did not have much of a plan except our route of driving there and an Airbnb for the first week to hit the ground running.

It took so much courage to do something like that. Reflecting on it now, I am like, *"how on EARTH did I do that?"*

I have the same thought when I think about my 16-year-old self who barely spoke English traveling alone to

England for the language course, or me at 21, moving to the US and leaving everything I knew behind.

**It blows my mind how much courage I embodied.**

The thing is, though, when you know something is right so deep within yourself, the fear does not stop you but in fact, fuels you. My heart felt so right after I got that download about going to LA that my whole body vibrated from enthusiasm. Then my mind, as the logical leader, started putting the necessary pieces together to keep us safe and have at least a plan if worse came to worst.

I ended up staying in LA for ten months, and it is still today one of the best years of my life.

## THE IMPORTANCE OF WALKING THE TALK FIRST

I wanted to share all of this as the introduction because **I believe that whatever you do, you must walk the talk.** Living by it first is the major part of being a practitioner, coach or guide of any kind. From these stories, I hope you now see how this lifestyle has been part of me ever since being young.

I want to mention one more heartful leap. While in LA, I pumped into the word of positive psychology while trying to think about what to do when I returned home. I found a

Master's degree in Applied Positive Psychology and Coaching Psychology that combined the science of wellbeing and coaching.

There it was again, the intense feeling in my heart that this was the science I had to study. In January 2019, I moved from LA to London and made another leap from journalism to psychology - to be able to not only write about people's stories but help people shape their stories and improve their wellbeing in whatever they might be experiencing.

This was my way of making a bigger difference beyond just writing and telling stories. I also knew that by improving humanity's wellbeing, suicide numbers would go down, too.

It did not make sense to many people why I would jump from journalism to an entirely different realm of study, but for me, it made every sense in the world. From the heartbreak of losing my brother and all it revealed to me, I found my purpose as a coach, connector, communicator and community builder. I found my purpose as a mental health and holistic wellbeing advocate to support people on their journeys - to help them go through the ups and downs of life, **to see the light at the end of the tunnel when the darkness hits hard and the tunnel seems never ending.**

**To help people see that heartbreak, pain and darkness we go through makes us find our higher purpose, why we are here and who we are meant to become** - just like it did for me.

It is part of being human and if I can help as many people to ride through all their tunnels to find their light in the end and find connection through it all - I have done my job.

I believe this philosophy of heartful, courageous living is a natural gift given to me by God, and it is this gift that I want to share with you now in this book. For you to understand the pillars of my philosophy of heartful living that I have proven to be true by embodying this daily and utilizing these methods and ideologies with my clients, groups, and workshop sessions.

The fact that you are here reading is a sign that you have followed your heart's calling, feeling this book is something you needed to read. Thank you for being here.

I applaud you for this because you have already taken what I call the intuitive action from the heart by getting this book. The first step into heartful living is to become aware of it and listen to your heart. The fact you are here is proof that you are at this stage and open to receiving.

So, welcome. I hope this little book will inspire you.

**I hope this book can guide you where you might face darkness and heartbreak, but not to allow it to break you down and rather break you open.**

**I hope this book will guide you toward a more connected life.** I hope this book will guide you toward a life:

Where your health is your most significant wealth and number one priority.

Where feeling energized and excited is part of your daily life.

Where you will lead and live an authentic life that feels like yours because your heart led you there.

Where adversity you go through is fuel for your empowerment and resilience.

Where you feel your best, so you can do your best.

Where you know "do your best and the Universe does rest" is enough.

Where you are living in harmony with your mind, heart, body, and soul.

Where you embody trust in yourself, others, the world, and something higher.

Where you gain a deeper understanding of yourself, others, this world and beyond.

And finally, where unconditional love is constantly present because you embody it. A place where love is easily accessed through the air you breathe and touched by every beat of your heart.

Welcome on this journey to living your version of a heartful life.

I cannot wait to see what that looks like for you.

# CHAPTER ONE
## H for HEALTH & HEALING

*"Keep connecting and keep moving - healing and health are a journey, not a destination."*
**— Essi Auguste Virtanen**

In 2020, I was attending a positive psychology webinar when I saw an illustration of someone's acronym on a specific subject matter. Their method popped up on my screen in which there was a word, and every letter stood out for something.

Something clicked in me and I just had to take my notebook, and this acronym came out of me like I knew it all along.

H - Health & Healing
E - Energy & Enthusiasm
A - Authenticity
R - Resilience
T - Trust
F - Fulfillment
U - Understanding
L - Love

It was all there. I had lived and coached through it, and it flew out of my pen with the most effortless flow.

Each element is the same as I originally wrote at that moment; only the deeper content, exercises, and elements have come together gradually the more I've reflected on this. Now, each element makes a chapter in this book.

So, the first part of my HEARTFUL method that I live by, guide, and coach my clients entails Health and within it, the essence of healing.

Everything starts from here. As I like to say: ***If you do not have your health, you have nothing.***

Similarly, if you do not heal yourself - physically, emotionally, psychologically, or spiritually - you are living a partial existence of being in separation within.

We live in a world of separation. Especially here in the Western world, so many things are separated. Even in our language, we separate everything.

A man and a woman. A mind and heart. Left and right. Black and white. Light and dark. However, **heartfulness is about oneness. Wholeness. The integration and connection between everything.**

To repeat what I quoted in the beginning of the book from my thesis study; *"... in the Eastern world heart and mind are often seen to describe 'the whole person' as 'one' and 'the center,' which sets the stage for mindfulness and heartfulness interconnectedness."*

**When we realize that we are all in connection within us, with each other and everything beyond that - we will find peace.**

The first step into the full realization, awareness, and embodiment of the whole way of being, in other words, heartfulness, is to check in with your health.

How I work with my clients is through flow. I do not plan, and this method does not always go in this particular order. Every human being is unique, and their journey is unique, so when it comes to this method, I usually flow in what aligns with the person's healing journey and where they are.

Often my clients approach me in one of these initial situations:

The overwhelm of change - feeling stuck in the head, unable to think clearly of what next. They are not being able to listen to the voice of their heart and intuition to make decisions and take actions to live their heartful fulfilling life. I hold space for them to find clarity within so they can action it externally.

Heartbreak - from a breakup to loss, individuals come to me when they are feeling broken, disconnected with themselves, with their people and the world around them. They come to coaching ready to start healing and start living their life after loss, finding meaning in it all and figuring out who they are after what they have experienced.

For me, the key is to connect to physical movement again. Two key states can occur while in heartbreak.

1. **Stagnancy:** You don't want to get out of bed or simply are unmotivated to do anything besides your responsibilities.
2. **Overwhelm:** You have no idea which direction to act toward as you are not hearing your intuition because you are disconnected within you. Your nervous system is simply in shock, so connecting and moving onward is difficult.

There is a lack of energy flow in both states, which means movement needs to be restored in the body so that energy can move within you, and, therefore, everything else in life.

***Where movement goes, energy flows.***

If we remain stagnant, then so does our mind. If we are overwhelmed and stay still with it, it will just stir within without releasing that energy.

With this disconnection, we must find a way to connect holistically in the body, mind, heart, and soul. And we start in the body because your body is the home of everything. The rest will start falling into place when energy flows in the body.

In 2017, when I was living in London after my brother's passing while doing my internship with CNN, a mantra appeared in my life that has served me ever since. It is a mantra that is overarching in every step of the HEARTFUL method.

*"Keep connecting. Keep moving."*

When in that state of pain, heartbreak, and disconnection, we must find a way to connect first; often, movement will naturally occur from that connection.

Whether it is movement of the body in a more physical exercise manner or movement just by taking action and moving through life, this is where we start. In this first stage, I support you **to find a way to connect with your body and move it, so energy can start flowing and life can start flowing again too.**

**Nothing moves or changes if you don't move.**

**I have this saying that we are not trees meant to be standing still, but beings meant to be in motion.** If there is a total lack of movement, our essence as human beings evaporate. I am not saying that we are not meant to have stillness - mindful, conscious stillness is needed for us to flourish to balance the motion in life.

However, when we are in the stagnancy where depression starts taking its power, we feel low and disconnected. That is because often, not much movement happens. If one is stuck in bed, one's energy and life feels stuck too.

There is a lot of science to back this up, and I believe in evidence-based practice because of my background in both coaching and journalism.

However, the purpose of this book for me is not to scientifically educate you about depression and disconnection but to present these issues simply - because when we simplify things, we can also find simple solutions and actions we can take. And I want you to have simple solutions that can support you on your journey to heartful living.

We often overcomplicate things, which can often prevent healing from starting. There is an overflow of information that we are surrounded with all the time, but it is taking action that will make the difference. There will be resources I will refer to in this book that you can dive in deeper, if resonates, but I want this book to be consciously more connection and movement focused. In other words, to be more reflection and action focused that anyone can have access to and action at any time.

I know every person's journey is multifaceted and complex, but I believe in the simplest of actions, positive change can be made. Not everyone has access to therapy, coaching or other forms of support - but with simple tools like I give in this book - I hope it can give you the extra assistance you may need to help you keep connecting and moving through what you are going through in your life.

**My belief system is that to heal depression, we must keep connecting within and moving ourselves somehow.**

It is about baby steps. I had a client who had gone through adversity and loss, and when we first started coaching, we came up with these two things for her to start her connection and movement practice.

**CONNECTION**: Writing an appreciation journal daily to find three things she appreciated and was grateful for to start connecting with what is good in her life versus just focusing on what was difficult. Where focus goes, energy flows, and if we only focus on the difficult, we just manifest more of that.

**MOVEMENT:** Doing two walks weekly in her neighborhood to get energy flowing.

In the beginning, even those two things seemed like the biggest things to do. However, by committing to those two actions, she gradually started feeling better, more connected and wanting to move in other ways in her life, too.

This was the starting point for us to be able to start working on other areas of her healing journey. Once we got her out of the stagnation to connect and move, this opened her energy and heart to do further work.

Honestly, connection and movement can be as significant as sitting up on the bed and taking a few breaths. **Breath is our life force that brings our heart and other organs to life.** Breathing gives us oxygen, making our heartbeat and other organs function in coherence.

**SIMPLE CONNECTION + MOVEMENT EXERCISE THROUGH BREATH**

Sit up and take six deep breaths for me. Put your hands on your heart to feel as it beats while you breathe. In the end, express your gratitude for your heart for beating through it all, and your body for keeping you moving through this time of your life. Express gratitude for your heart and your body, as they have been there for you through all the moments of your life.

Your body and your heart have your back.

**FIND YOUR CONNECT + MOVE ROUTINE**

The key thing is to start simple. To find your routine, reflect on these questions:

1. What simple way can I start connecting with myself every day?
2. How can I move my body in a simple way every week?

When we start small and simple, we set ourselves up for success, and when we feel success, the natural desire is to do more. If we start too big, it will overwhelm us and demotivate us.

**HOW I STARTED MY CONNECT + MOVE ROUTINE**

I want to give you an example of how I started applying these in my life to help you find what works for you.

After months of feeling so low after my brother's passing, I decided that every day I would find one happy thing.

Just *one.*

This became my connection point. I was so done feeling so low, so I made the commitment to search for one happy thing that happened each day and noted it in my planner.

Gradually, I started finding two, three, or four things per day, and at some point, realized that this feeling of happiness started to be more consistent in my life and within me.

As for movement, I had been a consistent gym goer but had lost the consistency while grieving. To help me keep moving and get back to the consistency, I got a personal trainer that I met with regularly who not only got me into good shape in the end, but she brought me back to life by coaching me on my mindset as well through some of the most challenging periods of my life.

**So, connecting and moving is where the path to heartful living starts.**

We can connect in many ways, but the key thing is to remember these three realms:

1.   Connecting with yourself
2.   Connecting with other
3.   Connecting with something higher

In any given moment, you can choose which form of connection you need the most. Sometimes it might be all three. For example, you might journal or meditate to connect with yourself. Then you might pray and finally call someone you love.

For me, back in 2017, it was journaling and talking to someone like I did with my trainer. My client journaled on three good things and had consistent sessions with me where I held space for her to process, heal, and take actions to prioritize her health.

**GUT IS YOUR CENTER - PRIORITIZE ITS HEALTH**

Of course, besides the above we also focused on other pillars of health, like nourishing and resting her body.

Let's touch on nourishing the body first. To start, I am not a nutritionist, but I want to share my experience, hoping it can give you ideas that might support you on your path to the best possible nutrition.

My life changed in 2023 when I could finally afford to do a test to find out my food intolerances.

**The gut is said to be our second brain.** How your gut is feeling will affect everything else in your body, from how your skin looks to your focus and energy levels and even chronic pain and migraines.

Most of my adult life I have suffered from bloating daily, even though I was working out 4-5 times a week, eating the basic fitness diet that included morning eggs, protein shakes, dairy yogurts, avocado toasts and alike. I barely drink alcohol. My biggest weakness in my diet had always been added sugar, which is the case for many. I mostly ate vegetarian and ate a lot of chickpeas and lentils for their great protein properties.

When I did this test in May, I found out I have a severe profile of intolerances, including everything I was eating daily: eggs, milk protein, gluten, yeast, chickpeas, lentils, peanuts, almonds, linseeds, and the list goes on.

I know, it is mental. I had to stop eating all of that. I had to let go of eggs and even PEANUT BUTTER. I was SO SAD at first.

Honestly, it was a shock, but at least now I knew that everything I was eating was not good for my gut. I had made a promise that whatever the test told me, I would cut all those foods to see what change I can see in my body. So, I did. I stopped all the above.

My self-regulation and discipline amaze me sometimes - this was one of those instances. I don't know how I did it because I had to stop everything I was used to eating daily and find a new routine. But I just wanted to feel better so much that if this was the answer, I was willing to do it.

So, what have I been able to eat? Rice, veggies, fruit, berries, natural fats and seasonings. I even brought fish, chicken, and pork back for protein intake, and honestly, my gut is the happiest it has ever been.

The vegetarian diet was not working as I was eating chickpeas and lentils that my gut was intolerant of. According to research from gut health experts, chickpeas and some beans can cause gut problems for many, so I encourage you to try going without those for a while and see how you feel.

Additionally, if you are vegan or vegetarian and eat a lot of the vegetarian/vegan equivalents, be aware that they can be ultra-processed and thus not helpful for your gut at all. Besides sugar, this is another major problem we have: We eat too many ultra-processed foods in today's world. So, if you take one thing out of this part of the book, please take this: start to eat more natural foods and less ultra-processed food. I promise that you will feel a change.

Again, I am not a nutritionist, I am just sharing my own experience having done the test and done a lot of research on this in the past year from several different gut health doctors out there. I have found that Dr. Vincent Pedre and Tim Spector are excellent in guiding us to living with a healthier gut, and I'd encourage you to familiarize yourselves with their work to support you on your journey.

I hope this helps you find what works for you. Every gut is different, and nutrition is one of those most multifaceted elements of being human that you must do the work to find out what works for you.

This is not about labels of being vegan, vegetarian, pescetarian, carnivore, or other. **I actually like flexitarian if we had to pick one - because everyone has to find their own flexible diet that works for them and their gut.**

**Our gut is literally our center. It is at the center of our whole body, so it reflects and affects everything in your body.**

**The ground rule for everyone is we must cut as much processed foods as we can - that is the one thing that is making us unwell in this world.**

The more natural, unprocessed, clean food you eat - the better you will feel. Guaranteed.

I mean, again, this is simple. Back in the early days of our human journey, we were hunting in the forest and eating berries and other things from nature, and that is how we are meant to eat today. We just have access to so much processed and unhealthy foods that this has become the norm - but you can make the decision for change today.

**I am writing this now in August, nearing three months without any of those foods I mentioned above, and I feel the best I have ever felt.**

The bloating and inflammation in my whole body is gone. My body is leaner. Fitness results are showing up better than ever before. My mental health and mood have improved with no actual low-mood days in the past three months. I am my most productive and focused. The number of headaches has decreased. I feel so good in my body; thus, my confidence and self-worth have also increased.

I know everyone might not have access to or be able to afford food intolerance tests - but to be conscious about what you are eating, noticing which foods sit well with your gut and which do not is the way to start. Become mindful about your eating. Then, simply make the choice to eat food that feels good and don't eat or minimize food that makes you feel bad.

Again, simple choices create long-lasting change. Sometimes the simple choice just seems hard when in fact that choice has the best interest at heart.

If you want to try to find out your food intolerances for free - there is a simple way although it can feel like a challenge. For 10-30 days, cut off the big food groups like dairy, grains, legumes, added sugar, alcohol and desserts. After the time period of your choice, you start to reintroduce a food group one by one to see which may set off any symptoms - depending on what symptoms you have experienced before.

What you can eat at this time is basically any clean food, including meat, seafood, eggs, fruit, veggies, and natural fats and seasonings.

Trust me, even cutting just grains or dairy for ten days, you will notice a difference in your body. So, you can even start with those two and see how it feels. However, may I note that because everyone's health is different, please consult your doctor to make sure whatever you choose to do is safe for you to try.

**How we nourish our bodies with nutrition directly reflects on how we can live our lives. This takes time, just like getting results with movement does.**

Positive changes take work - but this is the relationship with yourself, your gut, and your body we are talking about.

**Your body is your temple. If you do not have your health, you have nothing.**

**Your gut is your center - so make it a priority.** Find what works for you and do it - you will feel your best on the other side and that heartful aliveness is even more at your reach.

### SLEEP IS NON-NEGOTIABLE

Now that we have spoken about connection, movement, and gut health, I need to mention the importance of sleep.

**Sleep is the most underrated healer and one thing that many people sacrifice**. I am telling you now - sleep is the number one thing we must prioritize. Sleep is non-negotiable.

You cannot connect and move in your life if you are not well-rested. Rest also helps you process the food you eat to make the most of it.

I often say, *"rest is sometimes the best progress we can make."*

We must rest to balance all the doing. We must rest to recover from difficult experiences.

During my undergraduate years in college, I experienced a highly demanding environment, which could be described also as workaholic. I worked so hard that I started waking up from sleep and catching my breath in anxiety. This conditioning is still in me, and I need to stop myself sometimes so it does not start driving me. Workaholic hustling energy is that I am just in my head, not my body and heart. That is why we can feel anxious and get headaches, because we are literally working too HARD.

During my postgraduate degree and studying positive psychology in 2019, I learned that actually **I don't need to work "hard." I can work smart.** Working smart includes rest. I realized the more I allowed myself to slow down and rest, the more productive and more outstanding work I was producing and with more ease and less time.

Working smart also includes working in a way that aligns with our energy at the time. With women, this also links to our menstrual cycle. Depending on where we are in our cycle, we have different energy and thus perform differently.

That is why I advocate to raise awareness about periods in the workplace as this understanding can help leaders respect the women in their team. By honoring this natural cycle we have, we can perform our best, by not forcing our energy but working in alignment with where we are.

This honestly applies to anyone as some days you might plan to do a certain type of work but your energy aligns more with something else. Sometimes, if there is room for flexibility, changing your focus for the day can be most productive. Instead of forcing to do sales calls as your energy is really not there but getting all your admin done can be the best thing to do. **Honoring ourselves is where optimal performance is.**

However, I do acknowledge sometimes we must do what we don't feel like doing, and that is where discipline comes in, but this is just something to remember and keep in mind. **Honoring our energy is a massive asset for performance and getting the best results. When you honor your energy and follow your heart and gut - magical results happen. Often, even with less effort because the energy is so good that it manifests good results.**

Our world is a "doing" world, but we are human beings. When aligned in our being, we can be and do our best at work and in life. The more we force anything, the more resistance there will be.

As I mentioned, there are days we do not feel like doing something and must be disciplined, show up, and get it done. But there are ways we can align our energy to be our best. Even when we don't feel like it, we can tune in and realign and release resistance from within. We will discuss energy in the next chapter and how to optimize that.

So, to wrap this chapter, please prioritize these elements of health, and you will start seeing shifts in your life. I promise you.

1.   Allow healing and find space for it.
2.   Connect within, with others, and something higher.
3.   Move your body.
4.   Nourish your body in a way that works for your gut health.
5.   Prioritize rest and sleep.

**Health and healing are the beginning of becoming a whole and heartful you.** And to note: healing never ends. Healing is part of the journey of being human. This idea of a destination to "be healed" is nonexistent. The journey is healing, health, and growing through it all to attain our most heartful selves.

That is why healing and health are themes that will be with us throughout every element of the HEARTFUL method that we will cover in the rest of this book.

Whatever happens, I ask myself:

*"How do I need to connect through this? Do I need to connect with myself, someone else, or something higher? How can I move through this?"*

And whatever comes intuitively, I start there.

I will end the chapter with this: a mantra I return to for everything.

*Keep connecting and keep moving.*

I hope this mantra will serve you as much as it continues to serve me daily.

# CHAPTER TWO
# E for Energy &
# Enthusiasm

*"Enthusiasm is the electricity of life."*
**— Gordon Parks**

Energy is everything that we are. The air we breathe. The words we say. The emotions we experience. The connection we feel toward something or someone. The ideas we get. Everything we sense in this world.

**Everything is energy.**

In the previous chapter, we just discussed how important it is to keep moving because that is how you keep energy flowing in the body.

**When you move, so does energy within you.**
**When we are stagnant, so is our energy.**

Energy is carried in our bodies, and how we feel in the body affects what kind of emotional landscape we have, and vice versa.

However, there is one specific emotion which isn't talked about very much but it is the absolute key to heartful aliveness. This emotion is *enthusiasm.*

The Cambridge University dictionary defines enthusiasm as *"a feeling of energetic interest in a particular subject or activity and an eagerness to be involved in it."*

I am lucky that God gave me this gift that I am naturally and, by default, very enthused about life. However, this is not the case for everybody.

I am going to be frank with you, though:

**Something is not aligned and connected within you if you are not excited about your life. Period.**

Everyone deserves to be enthused about their life when they wake up. Yes, we all have low days too, which is part of life and its polarities.

To balance the light of enthusiasm, we need darkness too. We need the dark to appreciate the light we experience. It is part of our human existence.

**Embodying enthusiasm is a sign that energies are in harmony.**

To create harmony within ourselves, we need to tap into our energy body. This will enable us to see where blockages may have occurred which is preventing energy to flow throughout our bodies.

The system for this is called the Chakra System. As Cyndi Dale writes in her "Little Book of Chakras:" Chakras are energy organs within us that focus on all realms of our being: the physical, psychological, and spiritual.

When we access it we can discover something like a guiding system for us to tap into and find our highest energy self. When we are energetically in our highest, harmonious self, we can also live our life feeling our best and doing our best.

**The Chakra system consists of seven different energy centers:**

*Root*
*Sacral*
*Solar Plexus*
*Heart*
*Throat*
*Third Eye*
*Crown*

Each of the Chakra holds a particular aspect of our lives and has a space in the body dedicated to it.

Each Chakra holds a specific type of connection and realm of our existence, and altogether they hold the key for us to be optimally connected, thus healthy, and thrive in our lives.

**THE CHAKRA SYSTEM EXPLAINED**
I know to some of you this might be a bit out of the ordinary, so let me bring some science to explain this further.

There is physical energy like electricity that runs from power generation units through overhead lines into our households. That energy is measurable. However, this energy I am about to talk about related to the Chakra system is "subtle" and immeasurable.

As Cyndi Dale writes in her book: "Physically, emotions are created from electricity and chemicals through a complicated dance featuring the nervous system and endocrine glands."

Dr. Candace Pert, a scientist known for her mind-body work, "discovered that the cellular receptors for the nerves processing emotions are clustered at chakra points" (Pert, p. 245).

Chakras also are called as the "organs of light and sound" because every cell in our body radiates electrical charge or electrical field, electricity, in turn, creates a magnetic field, thus creating electromagnetic fields (EMFs), which in other words is called light (Dale, p. 36).

Similarly, all our organs and cells create a sound, which happens because vibration creates sound. Chakras respond to sound, which is why in Chakra meditations, we often hum a specific mantra that energetically realigns the Chakra with the correct frequency of sound.

Ok, are you still with me? I know that was a lot of information, but for those who seek science-backed information, I wanted to be sure to cover that because understanding is the first step to being able to apply it in your life.

To harmonize our energy and be able to feel fully embodied enthusiasm in our lives, connecting our energy through this system is key. So, how do we start?

To begin, let me break down the system for you and the different focuses and properties each Chakra has in a table form.

**THE CHAKRA SYSTEM AND ITS PROPERTIES**

| THE LEVEL | THE CHAKRA | THE LOCATION IN THE BODY |
|---|---|---|
| Physical | Root | Base of the spine |
| Psychological | Sacral | Lower abdomen |
| | Solar Plexus | Pit of the stomach |
| | Heart | Heart |
| Spiritual | Throat | Thyroid - Front of neck |
| | Third Eye | Forehead |
| | Crown | Top of the head |

*Table of Contents from Cyndi Dale "Little Book of Chakras:"*

## THE ROOT, SACRAL AND SOLAR PLEXUS: CONNECTION TO YOURSELF CHAKRAS

The Root Chakra, which is placed at the base of our spine, is about physicality, health, basic human needs, and your physical world. This is where everything starts.

What happens if you imagine a tree that would not be rooted anymore?

It falls over and loses its aliveness.

The same thing applies here.

If your root is not connected to the Mother Earth's physical realm, nothing will flow in the rest of your energy system.

This is why starting on the Root is key. To start on how you can move your body and focus on your physical health with movement, sleep, diet, and connecting to your environment. If your physical world and being are not settled, nothing else can be either.

Sacral Chakra, the second chakra in our system, is linked to our emotional being. This is the first chakra in the psychological realm. This again integrates with my process, as once the person feels more grounded and rooted in their physical world and body, they can tap into what they are feeling more and connect with themselves psychologically.

Once connected more with your emotional landscape, more openness and clarity toward mental action usually comes, which is the focus of Solar Plexus.

Home to our mindset and mentality, this is the Chakra where action is taken from. When we are connected to ourselves physically, emotionally, and psychologically, we can start taking action in the world more.

These three chakras hold what I call in my HEARTFUL system: "connection to yourself" work. When we do the work to connect and align these three chakras, we also feel more grounded and connected with ourselves. Once the energy here is established, we are more ready to connect with others.

The fourth chakra in the system is my personal favorite, the Heart Chakra. It is focused on self-love, love, relationships, compassion, and kindness. After doing the work on yourself and connecting with you first through the work of Root, Sacral, and Solar Plexus, we can move along to connect with others and start nourishing our relationships.

As the famous saying goes: "*You cannot love others if you don't love yourself first.*"

*My version is:* **You cannot connect with others profoundly, if you are not connected with yourself first.**

That is why many relationships crumble because people do not spend enough time connecting with themselves. We seek connection from the outside when that connection is impermanent and ever-changing. If you are disconnected with yourself, that disconnection is a mirror that reflects on your external relationships, too. We will touch on this a bit more in the final chapter when we talk about love.

That is why getting rooted within your physicality, connecting with your emotionality and the superpower of being you and your mentality are key.

**When you first learn who you are independently as *you*, that also changes your relationships with others for the better.**

**Healing starts from the body. Our emotions are kept in the body, and therefore, to make sense of them, we need to be more connected to the body first.**

**When we connect to our Root and Sacral landscapes, the Solar Plexus can then fire up, which is the home where emotion of enthusiasm resides.**

When we go through a difficult time in our lives, we disconnect and lose enthusiasm. That is why we must take it step by step - from the ground up.

Get rooted and grounded in your body and physical world.

Connect with your emotions - even the difficult ones - and give them space to be.

Connect with your mind and who you are now and act from it to awaken positive emotions and enthusiasm in your life again.

**THE HEART AND THROAT CHAKRA: CONNECTION TO OTHERS CHAKRAS**

**Once the three bottom energy centers and realms of your existence are connected, we can tap into the energy of the Heart Chakra. This is the home for compassion for our self and others, love and generosity.**

Above the Heart Chakra is the Throat Chakra, which is all about how you express yourself in the world.

After being in an unhealthy relationship back in 2020, it blocked my Throat Chakra. No matter how much I tried to communicate my truth, I was not heard, often ignored or neglected. This made me close up, and expressing myself in any way was difficult after this experience. I disconnected. I even took a break on Instagram back in the day as I really felt I had nothing valuable to say to the world.

However, having done deep healing work through coaching and therapy the last three years, my Throat

Chakra feels open again, and I am ready to write this book and express my truth and insights once again.

I am creating content again. And man, it feels good. Even though I am filled with fear writing this and thinking this is something that is soon open for the whole world to read - I am feeling the fear and doing it anyway, because I know in my heart that this book needs to be out there in the world.

**As I mentioned earlier, heartful living is courageous living.**

These two Chakras, the Heart and the Throat, are all about "connecting with others," the second realm of HEARTFUL practice.

**THE THIRD EYE AND CROWN: CONNECTION TO SOMETHING HIGHER**

The Third Eye, in the middle of our forehead, is all about our insights and vision. The more we feel like ourselves, the more we can envision and dream. Dreaming is an essential part of heartful living, but with the power of Solar Plexus below - you can take action on your dreams, too.

When we are connected and excited about life again, we can dream big and do bigger things as well. We are expressing ourselves in the world and have the power to share our insights with the world and make it a better place - in whatever form that may look like for you.

Maybe you share your insights by being a teacher, a parent, a friend, a speaker, or an author - the forms are endless.

I love the Third Eye because it is this bridge between connecting to others and the third realm of heartful practice, "connecting to something higher."

This energy center is about sharing what is real within you but also daring to dream and connecting with something higher and beyond ourselves that has yet to become a reality.

Finally, the Crown Chakra is located at the top of our heads. This is all about "connecting to something higher." In Maslow's hierarchy this would be linked to the highest phase of "transcendence."

*"Transcendence refers to the very highest and most inclusive or holistic levels of human consciousness, behaving and relating, as ends rather than means, to oneself, to significant others, to human beings in general, to other species, to nature, and to the cosmos"* (Maslow, 1971, p. 269).

In this state, you can have transcendent experiences of peace, joy, and fulfillment where you see things from a higher perspective and can feel this sense of "oneness" and "wholeness" within everything and everyone, which was one of my findings in my thesis study.

**According to my thesis study and the results I found in my research, heartfulness has three realms:**

1. *Connection to yourself;*
2. *Connection to others;*
3. *Connection to something higher.*

Having reflected on this beyond completing my studies, I made this connection to how these three realms link to the Chakra System, which we just covered. Here is the summary of them again:

**Connection to yourself - Physical, emotional, and mental existence**

      a.   Root
      b.   Sacral
      c.   Solar Plexus

**Connection to Others - relationship with yourself and others and expression of yourself in the world**

      d.   Heart
      e.   Throat

**Connection to Something Higher - Your vision for life and spiritual practice**

      f.   Third Eye
      g.   Crown

**HEARTFULNESS IS THE ENERGY OF ENTHUSIASM EMBODIED**

When we are enthusiastic about our lives, we are in harmony within the Chakra system. That is why it is vital to know about it, so we can observe as we go through life where there might be disconnection, and we can unblock it.

**This system is an essential part of my coaching practice and HEARTFUL philosophy.**

The last point I want to make is that **the system has seven Chakras, and the Heart Chakra connects the bottom three Chakras to the higher three.**

It is no coincidence. **The heart is the center of our being, where everything interlinks.**

**As the heart beats, that is our life force.**

**The heart is awakened by the connection of the three bottom Chakras, creating an endless flow of energy and heartful fulfillment, aliveness, enthusiasm, and sense of**

**oneness that expands beyond ourselves and others to something higher.**

## EXERCISE FOR CONNECTION: ENERGY CHECK-IN

Here is a little journaling exercise you can do to start connecting with your energy system to see which energy center/area of life might need more attention or unblocking for you to feel more energized in your life.

I created this questionnaire myself, and I use this when I take on a client as a tool to observe where the focus needs to be, and we measure changes as we go on.

### ROOT CHAKRA

1. On a scale of 1-10, how is your physical vitality currently? (1=very disconnected) (10= very good)

2. On a scale of 1-10, how grounded and secure do you feel in your life? (1=not at all) (10= very)

3. On a scale of 1-10, how safe do you feel financially? (1=not at all) (10= very)

### SACRAL CHAKRA

4. On a scale of 1-10, how much are you fueling your creative passions? (1=not at all) (10=a lot)

5. On a scale of 1-10, how connected do you feel with yourself? (1=not at all) (10=most connected)

**SOLAR PLEXUS CHAKRA**

6. On a scale of 1-10, how empowered and capable you feel about yourself achieving what you want in life? (1=not at all) (10=very much)

7. On a scale of 1-10, how much do you feel there is purpose in your work currently? (1=not at all) (10=very much)

**HEART CHAKRA**

8. On a scale of 1-10, how connected do you feel with other people? (1=not at all) (10=fully connected)

9. On a scale of 1-10, how happy are you about your relationships (friends, family)? (1=not at all) (10=the happiest)

10. On a scale of 1-10, how happy are you about your current romantic relationship status? (1=not at all) (10=the happiest)

**THROAT CHAKRA**

11. On a scale of 1-10, how truthful do you feel you are when you express yourself? (1=not at all) (10=very much)

12. On a scale of 1-10, how is the energy of the words you speak out loud? (1=very negative) (10=very positive)

## THIRD EYE CHAKRA

13. On a scale of 1-10, how clear do you feel about your vision for your future? (1=no idea) (10=the most clarity)

14. On a scale of 1-10, how much do your trust your intuition currently? (1=not at all) (10=totally)

## CROWN CHAKRA

15. On a scale of 1-10, how at peace do you feel currently within yourself? (1=feeling chaotic) (10=fully zen)

16. On a scale of 1-10, how connected do you feel spiritually/religiously? (1=not at all) (10=very connected)

## CONNECT WITH YOUR RESULTS

Check the ratings. Which ones are the highest? Which ones are the lowest?

This will give you answers where there is flow, blockages that need unblocking, and where your attention needs to go.

In my coaching, depending on the results, we explore them together and what came up for you doing the questionnaire. Then, we come up with a plan of action how we will go about our coaching and address the key themes and start realigning your energy system.

However, as I said, usually the Root Chakra is where to start because as I mentioned earlier: **if we do not feel rooted and grounded in our lives, nothing else can root and flow from there.**

**In my sessions, we also explore sources of enthusiasm because it is key to know where you can find it to create enthusiasm consistently in your life. Here's some questions for you to reflect on to get you started.**

*What makes you excited about life?*

*When was the last time you felt enthusiastic about something?*

*What were you doing? With whom? Where were you?*

To connect what makes us enthused about life is the key question - if we do not know, we cannot seek it. Observe where enthusiasm enters your body and reflect on what it is about it that is making you enthusiastic and how you can create more of that in your life.

Enthusiasm is heartfulness. Everyone deserves to be excited about their life. You just have to find what that looks like for you. You can lose sight of it, but you can always reconnect with it again by doing self-inquiry and possibly taking it to therapy or coaching, if that serves you on your journey. When you feel enthusiasm, you are connected to your authentic self. Let's talk about connecting to that next.

# CHAPTER THREE
# A for Authenticity

*"Authenticity is knowing who you are, and being that person in your daily life, awake and aware of your thoughts and feelings. Through heartfulness we become authentic one moment at a time in our thoughts, feelings, and actions."*

**— Stephen Murphy-Shigematsu**

As the quote says above, authenticity is to know who you are and being that person both through awareness and wakefulness - through it all. I mean the good and the pain, the light and dark, the good feelings and difficult ones - you allow all to be and do not escape the full experience of being you.

*"Authenticity means aligning your words with your actions and practicing what you believe and preach, without concern for what others may think of you."*

**— Stephen Murphy-Shigematsu**

We can catch people by not being authentic when they say something, but the action does not follow. This book is my way to walk the talk, to share stories of how I have lived this philosophy and continue to live it to this day.

**You are disconnected from your heart when you are not being your authentic self. Period.**

When I did my thesis study on heartfulness during my master's degree, I interviewed three yoga teachers about their understanding and experience of heartfulness and did an interpretative phenomenological analysis.

You can find a link at the end of this book to my website to download my thesis; if this is of interest to you to read as a whole.

*"Interpretative phenomenological analysis (IPA) is a qualitative approach which aims to provide detailed examinations of personal lived experience. It produces an account of lived experience in its own terms rather than one prescribed by pre-existing theoretical preconceptions and it recognises that this is an interpretative endeavor as humans are sense-making organisms." (Smith, & Osborn, 2015).*

I chose this method because I have always been about lived experiences as a journalist, and in-depth interviewing and analysis of the yoga teachers' narratives felt right in pursuit of answers.

As I've mentioned before, three grand themes came out in my study: connection to yourself, others, and something higher. One of the concepts that revealed itself within the first theme of "Connection to yourself" was authenticity.

**To have the courage to follow your heart to live an authentic life that feels like yours and where you are following your heart's callings.**

According to Dr. Stephen Joseph in his book "Authentic," there are three elements to authenticity.

*Know yourself*
*Own yourself.*
*Be yourself*

On his website, knowing yourself is defined as:
*"Authentic people know themselves. They are able to listen to their inner voice, and they can understand the complexities of their feelings. To be authentic, we need to be able to face up to the truth about ourselves, no matter how unpleasant we might find it."*

This links to my process during the Sacral Chakra period of aligning our energy when it is all about knowing what is emotionally going on with you. **It is hard for us to deal with difficult and unpleasant emotions.** All we want is for that feeling to go away. The funny thing is **the quicker you allow yourself just to feel it and be in it, you also free yourself from it.**

It is painful to connect with the traumatic and hurtful events, but **when we courageously do that, we get to know ourselves and who we are after going through those experiences.**

In my coaching and groups, I hold space for people to connect with what they have gone through and how it is making them feel to start verbally processing it and giving it space. That is step one - just start talking about it.

I remember on the day my brother died - I remember just going from one close friend to another and repeating the same events when I got the phone call about my brother's passing. Talking about it repeatedly and just repeating the event helped me process it.

The quicker you can do this, the better, as it is a way for you to process and be in the experience. Saying what has happened out loud can be the biggest step in coming to terms with what happened. For some, doing that might even take a while because saying it out loud makes it feel more real.

**Facing and accepting what has happened in your life, no matter how difficult the truth may be, is the first step to connecting with yourself authentically.**

I never said heartful, authentic living is easy.

## MY JOURNEY WITH EMDR THERAPY

Having been in talking therapy on and off for a few years, in the spring of 2023, my therapist recommended I pursue EMDR therapy. According to the British Association for Counseling and Psychotherapy, "EMDR stands for Eye Movement Desensitisation and Reprocessing, a form of psychotherapy that helps you process and recover from past experiences affecting your mental health and wellbeing."

She said having talked about the traumatic events extensively through the years, it was time for me to go in and actually feel them.

No matter how much you process your traumas in your mind, the trauma is within your body.

EMDR involves using side to side eye movement with talking therapy in a very controlled, structured manner. It opens your subconscious mind to process difficult or traumatic memories. You go through the process of memory by memory, starting from the least painful one and working toward the most traumatic one - all while releasing emotions and beliefs associated with those memories stuck within your body.

EMDR was pure magic for me. Every memory we worked through and the negative connotations I had around them were released in a matter of 20-30 minutes per memory. It took me 7 sessions to release everything I felt was important.

My thoughts and beliefs about the memories that were overpowering and painful are just not there anymore. They are now just memories I have without the overpowering, paralyzing, tense effect on my body and mind.

I have never felt freer.

**Whatever you have gone through, you must feel it to free it.**

It is scary - don't get me wrong. I was anxious for the weeks leading up to it, but even that anxiety I experienced was my body telling me it knew what was coming.

EMDR helps you find and see from a new perspective, create more positive beliefs over the negative ones, and set you free from any mental or physical symptoms you might be having.

I am not saying EMDR is suitable for everyone, but I encourage everyone to find a somatic approach that feels right to them. If you are someone who has been in talking therapy for a while now, adding a somatic approach will be a gamechanger.

You can talk about these things all day, but if you don't feel and release it from your body - it stays there.

**OWN YOURSELF - TAKING RESPONSIBILITY**

The next stage of authentic living is to own yourself. It is about taking responsibility and accountability for your life and knowing you can create your own reality.

We all are in the victim mindset sometimes, but when we dare to face ourselves and our role in any scenario, freedom lies on the other side, and positive change can occur.

If you think everything in life happens to you and not for you, you get stuck in this victim mindset. When you start to see everything in life happen for you, you awaken the empowered being in you who can own their life.

You get to decide whatever happens to you and what you will do with it.

*How are you going to view it? How are you going to respond? What are you going to make of it?*

**Our greatest pain, heartbreak, and darkness are our greatest teachers of giving us what we need to be our best selves in this world. If we start to see that difficult things that happened are *for* us to tap into the potential in disguise, our lives will change.**

So, own it. Own whatever happens for you. In everything, you play a role, own it.

One of my favorite quotes of all time goes:

*"Life will present you with people and circumstances to reveal where you're not free."*

**— Peter Crone**

**Everything that happens for you is meant for you to go through.** God never gives us anything we are not strong enough to go through. Everything given to us is a pathway to freedom.

**Every experience and human being is a mirror of ourselves, showing what we need to see.**

*How would your life change now if you looked at your experiences through this lens?*

**KNOWING AND UNDERSTANDING THE GOOD SIDE OF OURSELVES**

Besides facing and feeling the difficult experiences and owning ourselves, we also need to know and understand the good within us.

This links to what I asked at the end of the previous chapter: *What makes you excited about life? What do you like in life and about yourself? What do you enjoy doing? What do you want? What do you dream about?*

All of these questions are key in getting to know yourself.

Part of this is to get to know your strengths and values.

**BEING YOURSELF THROUGH STRENGTHS AND VALUES**

The last element of being your authentic self, according to Dr. Joseph's model, is being yourself.

Besides facing the good and the bad within us, you also need to understand what you value and where your limits are to be able to be yourself.

**You need to know and own your values and boundaries.**

**How are you expected to live an authentic life if you do not know your strengths, what you value in this life, and what you are ok and not ok with?**

In this world, you can be pushed to be someone you are not, but when you connect with yourself deeply and get to know and own yourself, you find that courage in your heart to pursue a life that feels rightfully yours.

**The external noises can get to you, but nothing can stop you when you have your inner intuitive voice louder.**

**I bring values and strengths to the coaching space to support people to reconnect with their authentic selves.** Without connecting with your values and strengths, you cannot know who you are and be that.

Our values and strengths help root us and know where we stand in this world. **We can set better boundaries and understand what is for us and what is not. They are like a guiding post for you to make choices that are right *for you*.**

When you connect and start living by your strengths and values, you will become a magnet to what you want in this life, and the Universe will support you in your journey to be the heartful version of you.

This is where people start to gain clarity. When the value system is clear, it becomes clear to them what really matters, and answers can be found. Additionally, when people connect with their strengths within, which we have at all times, it empowers them. This part is one of my favorites as this is where a person will reconnect with themselves and feel like themselves once again.

**CONNECTING WITH YOUR STRENGTHS EXERCISE**

The easiest way to get started on this by yourself is to do the Values in Action questionnaire, which is free and online.

https://www.viacharacter.org/

In positive psychology character strengths are defined as built-in capacities for particular ways of thinking, feeling, and behaving (Linley, 2008). This assessment will give you a profile of 24-character strengths you have actioned on. We all have these strengths, but our profiles vary. The top ones on the list are strongest within you at the time you completed the assessment, and the bottom ones are strengths you have actioned least.

These 24 strengths are within you always, just in different degrees, and can give you profound answers on how to be in this world in a way that feels right to you. This assessment has been well researched, and these 24 strengths are acknowledged across the world through various cultures. The strengths are divided into 6 virtues. Here is the breakdown of all of them for your benefit:

**Wisdom**

- Creativity
- Curiosity
- Love of learning
- Open-mindedness
- Perspective

**Courage**

- Authenticity
- Bravery
- Persistence
- Zest

**Humanity**

- Kindness
- Love
- Social intelligence

**Justice**

- Fairness
- Leadership
- Teamwork

**Temperance**

- Forgiveness
- Modesty/Humility
- Prudence
- Self-regulation

**Transcendence**

- Appreciation of beauty and excellence
- Gratitude
- Hope
- Humor
- Religiousness/Spirituality

What I want to bring to your attention that links to my method beautifully. You can see that strengths of authenticity, bravery, persistence and zest are underneath the virtue of Courage. This showcases how heartful living,

living as your authentic self from your heart space takes courage.

In the previous chapter, we spoke about enthusiasm, and zest strength means: "approaching a situation, or life in general, with excitement and energy, not approaching tasks or activities halfway or halfheartedly. People who are high in zest are excited to get up in the morning, and they live their lives like an adventure."

This bridges the elements of authenticity and enthusiasm/energy from the HEARTFUL method beautifully, and how strengths and values are necessary aspects to live a courageous, heart-led life.

Finally, guess what is the one way to know if one is using their character strengths in their life just by observing people? Enthusiasm - when the person expresses enthusiasm and excitement for their life, character strengths are in action. If a person does not, it is likely they are disconnected from their inner strengths.

Positive psychology recognizes that each one of us is stronger in some areas and less strong in another, and that is what makes each of us beautifully unique and human. It is a beautiful framework helping you to connect with your authentic self and find more enthusiasm in your life.

Even if you don't go do the assessment, you can ask yourself and journal on these questions:

*From that list above: Which I feel are my top five strengths and which ones I feel I am less strong at this time? Which one of these values listed are important to me? Which are less important?*

Doing this kind of self-inquiry will improve your self-awareness and help identify where improvement needs to happen.

This can give you the starting point to connect what you value in your life and what values are stronger in action within you, and what authentic being means to you.

I do this assessment every six months as the profile will change depending on what values I am focusing on and actioning on in that time of my life. This is a wonderful tool to have a look at which areas of strengths are really strong within me and which areas I need to focus on to live more heartfully and aligned.

In my coaching, I do a special 1.5-hour values session where, through your own narrative and stories, I run through a process where you will have your own core ten values to live by the end of the session. Then we compare the results of VIA and your own and expand our exploration of you at your authentic self through further strengths identification.

This is a deeply empowering work that combines the power of your personal stories, this area of positive psychology, the power of values for you to tap into your authentic self, and enthusiasm to live more courageously from your heart.

When you know your values and strengths - you stand stronger than ever and are able to set limits to honor yourself. Let's talk about that next.

**QUICK ONE ON BOUNDARY SETTING**

Boosted by the strengths in you and knowing your values; boundaries need to be set.

The more healing you do, the more you notice your standards increase, and your awareness of what you will and will not tolerate increases. When you know your values - this also opens the dialogue to what your boundaries are. Usually, we explore boundaries in a specific scenario when connecting with others, including romantic relationships, family, or friendships.

**You can get started with these journal prompts.**

*What are deal breakers for you?*
*What is a whole-embodied NO that you will not tolerate under any circumstance?*
*What is a whole-embodied YES that you want more in your life?*

*What else is important to you in connecting with others that you need to feel your best within you?*

Even though boundaries are linked to connecting to others' realm of heartful living - setting and holding our boundaries is actually still more about the way we love and respect ourselves. It is not others' responsibility to hold your boundaries - it is yours. Therefore, boundary setting and holding to them is part of owning who you are.

I leave you with this:

*"Daring to set boundaries is about having the courage to love ourselves even when we risk disappointing others."*
**— Brené Brown**

Never love others more to let go of your values and boundaries. Always love and respect yourself first - even if that means disappointing others.

## HEARTFUL AUTHENTICITY IN FOUR STEPS

To summarize what we have covered in this chapter, these four steps must be taken to connect with yourself authentically.

1.  Connecting with and feeling your journey, what you have gone through, and who you are after those experiences - both the good and the painful

- and courageously embracing and being you, and not caring what others think.
2. Taking responsibility for your role in everything - owning yourself.
3. Connecting with your strengths to get to know and be your authentic self and tap into more enthusiasm in your life
4. Connecting with your values and setting boundaries that align them.

Additionally, a simple question of: *"which strength or value can help me in this current phase of my life?"* can be the most profound moment of connection, which can help boost resilience, find solutions, and help you keep connecting and keep moving forward in your life.

We will talk about that next.

# CHAPTER FOUR
# R for Resilience

"七転び八起き

*Nana korobi ya oki*

*Fall seven times, rise eight.*"

— **Japanese proverb**

To start our exploration about resilience, I must remind you of something we covered earlier. We started the journey with a letter H which stands for health and healing. As I mentioned, health is the foundation for being human, because without our health, we have nothing. Additionally, our journey in this life is meant for us to optimize our journey in our bodies, minds, and souls - holistically - and that is the healing part.

Life often challenges us with difficulties, adversity, pain, and heartbreaks. Healing from them is part of our human journey, and to remind you, it is not about the destination of being "healed." We are always healing, as we are always growing and evolving, day by day, aiming to find inner peace and equilibrium with what we have gone through so we can be most fully ourselves through everything we experience.

**An important part of this growth, evolution, and healing is *resilience.***

Resilience is the part where we talk about the adversity you have gone through in your life. When it comes to my coaching, this part is the part that is hard to get into, face and connect over.

However, healing the wounds in our hearts is a key part of living a heartful life.

*It is the scars in our hearts from the heartbreaks we have gone through that are the answer to who we are meant to become. It is those scars that are the map for us to find our path to fulfillment and purpose.*

As I said at the beginning of this book, I work with clients by intuitively flowing with what they bring. Usually, what brings individuals to coaching with me is they have faced a form of adversity, loss, or heartbreak. They reach out because **they want to reconnect with themselves and their life, and figure out who they are now after that experience.**

Often with my clients, we do start with the health, enthusiasm, and authenticity realms - just to focus on reconnecting and getting to know them again and changing the energy within them. As the energy in their body and mind shifts, a different perspective of what has happened can surface, and gradually this works gets them to a more rooted and connected place to be ready to talk about what has happened a bit more in depth. However, every human is different, and sometimes the order does shift as everyone's process of reconnecting with themselves is different.

## RESILIENCE IS NOT BOUNCING BACK; IT IS BOUNCING FORWARD.

Overcoming such an adverse event is often referred to as "bouncing back" to the normal state of functioning in positive psychology literature. However, I want to bring up Dr. Taryn Marie Stejskal, who is the world's leading resilience and mental health expert, who brings up the idea that rather than "bouncing back" it is about "bouncing forward."

Dr. Marie states resilience is built within us throughout our lives with the challenges, changes and complexities that are put our way.

I love Dr. Marie's way of looking at this because when we really think of it, It is impossible for us to bounce back to what was or who we used to be because we are no longer the same person we were then. Yesterday was yesterday. We change every single day. **Therefore, we can only**

**bounce and move forward with our lives as we are after what we have experienced.**

**So, my mantra of "keep connecting and keep moving" connects to this as we have to remember to connect with ourselves through the changes, challenges, and complexities of life and take active actions and move through it all.**

**This is among the most important connection work one can do.** This is also often where, if someone has gone through very traumatic events in their past, I might recommend them to pursue therapy alongside coaching with me to make sense of those stories from the past, and how they affect the present, so they can untie those knots and find more freedom in the present and in their future.

Resilience in a positive psychology context is defined: "*the capacity to remain flexible in our thoughts, feelings, and behaviors when faced with life disruption, or extended periods of pressure, so that we emerge from difficulty stronger, wiser, and more able*" (Pemberton, 2015, p. 2).

How do we do that? We tap into our own personal resources. Positive psychology resilience research states these are the six key factors in resilient individuals (Boniwell & Tunariu, 2019; Neenan, 2018), which are presen in the HEARTFUL method. I will illustrate how these show in my method, using their original titles of the factors.

1. **"Reframing"** - In my words, the "new perspective" that comes can support you in what you are going through to help you keep connecting and moving through it.

2. **"Using the power of positive emotions"** - When we look for positives in our lives, even in the smallest way, we open the door for more of that. This is where the appreciation list exercise from Chapter One comes in handy. If I find something I appreciate every day, then I create more things that I can appreciate.

3. **"Participating in physical activities"** - Keep moving your body. Next to finding something positive, it is key to move the body to improve how you feel. As we also learned in the first chapter.

4. **"Ongoing active engagement in trusted social networks"** - We cannot do this alone. Having a support system around you is key to keep moving, to avoid isolating yourself in your pain, and connect through it and feel you are not alone. When we connect with others, the sense of togetherness itself heals, and by having trusted

people around you, they can help with factor 1 "reframing" of what happened and find a new perspective in the journey.

5.  **"Identifying and using signature strengths"** - We mentioned this in the previous chapter. When we connect to our strengths, we feel more authentically ourselves, we get to know ourselves, and we know how we can be ourselves again. With our strengths, we are fuelled to face life, its changes, and challenges going onward.

6.  **"Optimism regarding the future"** - All of the above, when in motion, can help us tap into optimism, which in turn awakens more hope and positivity about the future.

All of these six elements are important in resilience and connecting with it. However, I want to focus a bit more on the very first element: "reframing," in my words, a perspective shift.

When we go through something which can be quite a significant traumatic event in our lives, they not only make us more resilient in life but can also give us a new perspective toward life, a new meaning, and purpose.

**This is what I call "turning your pain into purpose."**

**This is when powerful heart-led human beings come to be.**

I am here writing this book today, living my purpose of heartful living because it is fuelled by the loss of my brother who passed away way too soon. I wish he was here with us, but the best thing I can do is to use the pain of loss and turn it into meaningful, purposeful work wanting to help people to see there is always light at the end of the tunnel. I could not help my brother, but I hope I can help many others.

**Heartful living is to be a resilient, courageous warrior of a human who keeps rising up after they fall, feels their pain and uses that pain for the highest good for all.**

The pain and adversity you face at the end of the day happens for you, no one else, because you are strong enough to go through it. It is here to test you to become your best self. **Our adversity has the power to unlock our heartfulness, but only if you do the healing so you are able to make sense of it all and who you are becoming in the process.**

Loss, adversity, and heartbreak change us, and as we change, we see the world entirely differently, so we have to connect with who we are after that.

**We must meet ourselves again, get to know ourselves again, and understand what it is that keeps us going through it all.**

I hope through my work as a coach and community builder I can guide people to become heart-led resilient individuals who feel free and can keep on moving forward in their life and turn their pain into a powerful purpose.

However, it is very hard to think if you are in the midst of a very challenging, traumatic time period right now as you are reading this, "Okay, cool, I just will turn this worst experience of my life into purpose now."

It does not happen just like that.

Healing takes time and has its stages. We have to grieve the change, loss, and challenge that we have gone through.

**THE FIVE STAGES OF GRIEF**

You might have heard about the five stages of grief. This is work advocated by Elisabeth Kübler-Ross and David Kessler. The steps are:

1. **Denial -** denying of what has happened.
2. **Anger -** being angry about what has happened.

3. **Bargaining -** living the "if only, what ifs" - remaining in the past, trying to negotiate your way out of the hurt.
4. **Depression -** This is getting present with the pain, after spending the past in bargaining. The hurt hits you, and it gets real.
5. **Acceptance -** You find acceptance for what has happened.

As we grieve, we go through these phases in different ways. It is also not a step-by-step process, but we go through these stages repeatedly. One day, you feel you are in acceptance; the next, you are angry about it and bargaining your way, and the next, you deny it all. Now you might be utterly sad about it. Sometimes you might go through all these stages in a day. Every day is different, and grieving is not linear.

When I heard about my brother in 2017, I went to the classic denial straight after my mom had told me.

*"No, they got this wrong. They have mixed my brother with someone else."*

Then the depression hit me, and I lost feeling in my knees and fell to the ground and just screamed. It did not take long, and as I was sharing about it during that first day, I found myself bargaining and just wanting to avoid the hurt with "what ifs."

*"What if we had been there? What if I had talked to him more?"*

It is all part of the journey, and it took me months to get to the slightest level of acceptance, but only six years later, after the EMDR therapy I did in 2023, I profoundly found peace with it all.

**Healing and grieving take time. Give yourself time and honor your journey.**

I want to highlight this: Nobody has the right to tell you how to grieve or when to be done with grieving. No grieving process is the same, and your grieving is yours. **The grieving also never ends, just like healing never does; it just eases with time and can come in waves unexpectedly.**

**Healing and grieving are these beautiful partnered essences within us throughout our lives.**

That is why normalizing talk about grief is important to me. We need to understand that grief is part of our lives and something to see in each other's experiences and allow people to go through the stages at their own pace.

**THE SIXTH STAGE: FINDING MEANING**

David Kessler also wrote another book with Elisabeth Kübler-Ross called "Finding Meaning: The Sixth Stage of Grief."

This brings home my philosophy of turning your pain into purpose.

Kessler stated that finding meaning takes you beyond the five stages and can "*transform grief into a more peaceful and hopeful experience.*"

When we find meaning and purpose in what was lost - we find inner peace, hope, and eventual heartfulness.

As we near the end of this chapter, I have one yet very important thing I want to say about grieving.
Grieving does not happen only with major traumatic events, loss, or death. Grieving can be about mourning the old version of you. Grieving can be leaving a place behind when moving somewhere new. Grieving can be about "what could have been."
Grief takes many forms, big and small.
**Grief can even be about a single moment that was missed.**

This next part, pay extra attention. This is one of those that really can change your life, if practiced in your life.

**JAPANESE WISDOM OF ICHI-GO ICHI-E**

This principle from Zen Buddhism is attributed to a sixteenth-century master of the Japanese tea ceremony, or "ceremony of attention," to focus on the present moment. It is about "this time only" and "once in a lifetime."

In my own words, ichi-go ichi-e captures the essence of mindfulness and heartfulness together so that **this moment is now and will never come again, so let's fully embrace it with our whole-embodied, heartful presence.**

In today's world, it is easy to live in the future thinking about what we want to accomplish or ruminate about our past events. That is why we often miss the present moment, which is the greatest loss.

*"Life can only take place in the present moment. If we lose the present moment, we lose life."*
**— Buddha**

**The biggest regret we can have is to experience a moment, only to realize afterward we were not there, and we missed it.**

And we can never get it back. That is where grief can happen in its purest form and which we do not talk about enough - **the loss of what was but which can never be again. It was only once in a lifetime, that moment only.**

I have a profound love and connection to Japanese philosophies, where they appreciate this fleeting nature of life in its impermanence. **Ichi-go ichi-e is about every moment being this gift that we know fleets away - so we must cherish them to the fullest.**

My favorite Heartfulness practitioner, Stephen Murphy-Shigematsu, writes about this in his book "From Mindfulness to Heartfulness: Transforming Self and Society with Compassion:

*"If we can consider the reality that every encounter is one of a kind, and therefore something to be treasured as if it is the one time in our life, we will value the time. Approaching life in this way, we will have an abundance of enriched moments."*

**That is what I want for you, my dear reader. To not miss any moments but to have an abundance of enriched, heartful moments that you treasure fully when they happen and can remember vividly for the rest of your life.**

## HEARTFUL HIGHLIGHTS EXERCISE

We created and printed our own Connected planner with my friend Tamara Judge who also is a positive psychology practitioner and coach. In this planner, besides weekly scheduling, you can coach yourself through positive psychology and personal development prompts to live a more connected life.

In this planner, we have a section called **"Heartful Highlights" after every month where you can reflect and savor moments that really enriched and fulfilled your heart.** It is a space for remembering moments and a beautiful way to practice ichi-go ichi-e.

I would encourage, whether you have our planner or not, to practice this. Jot down heartful moments in your journal, calendar, or your note app on your phone. Having moments written like this is an excellent way to practice gratitude, savoring, and it can work as a reminder of what a beautiful, heartful life you are living with moments to cherish.

This is a beautiful "bounce onward" exercise to boost resilience as well when you are having a challenging time. Just open up your heartful moments page and it will remind you about all the good in your life that can boost you to keep connecting and moving forward in your life.

## SEE THE RESILIENCE WITHIN YOU - REVERSE BUCKET LIST EXERCISE

I love this exercise from Dr. Taryn Marie Stejskal which is similar in nature to the Heartful Highlights but looks at your life from a bigger picture. We often write about the bucket list of what we want to do in our lives, but this exercise is about recognizing and journaling on the things you have already gone through. **Write down all the challenges you've conquered but also successes and great things in your life that you have accomplished.**

This exercise is an excellent illustration to show how much resilience you have within you, note how far you have come in life and to show you how much experience you have to trust yourself to follow your heart to live your own version of a courageous, fulfilling life.

## RESILIENCE IN SUMMARY

1. Resilience is courage to face what we have gone through and reconnect with who we are after that experience and getting to know ourselves again.
2. Heartful resilience is about bouncing onward, not bouncing back.
3. Resilience is about keep connecting and keep moving through it all.
4. Grieving and healing are part of our life.
5. Grieving takes many forms and your process is yours only.

6.   Embrace the present moment fully, and you will have an abundance of heartful richness to remember and boost your resilience through challenging times.

We need to grieve what was lost in order to heal our hearts to be able to see the other side - the side where acceptance settles in, meaning is found and trust in yourself and everything on your journey can ignite.

We will speak about trust in the following chapter.

# CHAPTER FIVE
# T for Trust

*"You need to find the courage to trust the wise counsel of your heart, even at moments of disappointment and sadness. Then you can begin to truly believe that a setback is not the end of the world, but can actually bring about an interesting turn in your life."*

**— Baptist de Pape**

The more I connect with this chapter, the more I think this is actually probably one of the most important parts of heartful living. It is simple in essence but can feel like the most challenging thing to do.

Trust, for me, links to your belief system, in yourself and others, and something higher. Earlier in this journey, you have connected with your values and strengths, which link to this. When we are connected to ourselves and what we stand for, trust also strengthens.

So, my dear reader: *What do you believe in?*

Back in 2017 when I lost my brother, that was a moment where I believe my faith system really activated.

When you go through something that heartbreaking that does not make any sense.
When you lose someone to suicide, there are often unanswered questions.
You don't have tangible proof; that is where surrendering to something beyond comes in.

When nothing makes sense in this realm, you can always lean on something higher.

First, I leaned on my belief system: "*Everything happens for a reason. Everything happens for a reason. There is a reason why this has happened. Keep going.*"

I just wrote in the previous chapter how it would take time to find purpose and meaning in the adversity, loss, and heartbreak we go through. During the first months after my brother's passing, when I was still very far from acceptance and deep into the depression of it all, holding on to this belief that everything happens for a reason was like a guiding light at the end of the tunnel that I was slowly making my way toward.

*"One day, I will understand why this happened."*

If you have a strong belief system, your trust in yourself, others, something higher, and life itself strengthens. These three pillars of trust are key to heartful living:

**THREE PILLARS OF TRUST**
*Trusting yourself*
*Trusting others*
*Trusting something higher*

This again links to the three themes I concluded in my thesis study.

*Connection to yourself*
*Connection to others*
*Connection to something higher*

**Once we feel connected, trust sets in.**
**If there is disconnection, trust cannot exist.**

Iyanla Vanzant, in her book "Trust - Mastering the Four Levels of Trust" writes about trust in a way that really connects with my method. She notes that mantra for successful living is:

*"Trust yourself, Trust God, Trust others and Trust in life."*

She writes how we trust from the moment we take our first breath in this world as a baby. Life is all about trust.

**We trust our heart to beat and our body to function.** We trust our parents to care for us as babies as we cannot do it ourselves.

We just trust - there is no question because we don't know anything else. Trust is there - always.

**Iyanla also states that trust is the simplest thing to do but still the hardest to master.**

It is key to master it, though, as if we don't, we end up feeling stuck, or in my vocabulary, feeling disconnected from ourselves, others, our lives, and something higher.

Iyanla wrote so beautifully about trust and connection to the heart that I wanted to share it with you:

*"Until and unless you master these four levels of trust, your heart will be at risk. It will become brittle, broken, hardened, and embattled. It will be prone to attack you and everyone else. When you do what is required to develop and deepen your trust in these four areas,* openhearted, lighthearted *and* clear-hearted *are the words that will describe the fruits of your labor."*

Iyanla writes, when we master trust in these key realms - we feel "guided, protected, enlightened, and fulfilled."

**So, how do we work on our trust?** Well, everything starts with the connection and trust in yourself. The rest will not fall into place if you do not have that. This goes back to the energetic body we discussed in Chapter 2. You cannot stand strong and solid within yourself if you are not rooted in your lower energy centers.

**Trusting yourself is all about hearing and listening to your inner guiding system, gut feeling, and heart callings.**

**Trusting others is all about keeping your heart open and trusting people in your life.**

**Trusting something higher is about what I call the practice of surrender and letting go and letting God.**

Let's visit each of these realms, and hopefully, this will give you a good starting point to start your self-inquiry about where you are with your connection with trust.

**CONNECTING EXERCISE: INQUIRY ABOUT YOUR BELIEFS AND TRUST**

A good exercise for this to start is to simply journal on these questions:

*"What do I believe in?"*

*"Why do I believe that?"*

**Our beliefs are like our anchors. Similar to strengths and values, when you add beliefs in the mix, you feel so anchored in your being that no matter the waves that will hit it, you are unshakeable.**

**SCALE YOUR TRUST**

I use scaling a lot in my coaching as it gives an interesting landscape to explore where we are and start a conversation.

*On a scale of 1-10, how strongly do I feel I trust myself?*
*On a scale of 1-10, how strongly do I feel I trust others?*
*On a scale of 1-10, how strongly do I feel I trust something higher?*

Whatever scores you receive, it will give you answers in what realm your trust seems stronger and where less strong and it can guide you to some profound answers to explore with yourself or even take into coaching or therapy space. Usually, there is a specific realm that might be stronger than others.

With the one where you might lack trust, ask yourself:

*How was this trust broken?*
*What is standing in the way for me to trust in this realm?*

**Usually, when there is disconnection with trust, the trust has somehow been broken. Looking at the root cause of where the trust was broken is key to being able to build your trust again.**

**Rebuilding trust is not easy work. Like the other elements of HEARTFUL living - it takes courage, vulnerable authenticity, connection and committed action.**

This quote summarizes this perfectly:

*"Once trust is broken it is like a crumpled piece of paper, you can try to smoothen it over, but it will never be fully the same."*
**— Unknown**

This is true. That trust will never look the same, but you can recreate the sense of trust with who you are after that experience.

Again, as I stated in Chapter 4, resilience is not about bouncing back, but it is about bouncing forward. The same thing applies here. **Trust cannot be bounced back, but you can bounce it forward and recreate what trust in a specific realm looks like for you.**

I believe it is the biggest weight we can carry in our hearts is to mistrust because of an experience we have lived through.

**None of the painful and challenging experiences you go through are worth losing your trust in yourself, others, and something higher.**

Never allow anyone or anything to take away that. Because when we were babies, we just trusted the world and surrendered. That is freedom. People lose that freedom with conditioning; these experiences, fear and pain we all go through, but we do not have to.

No matter what happens for you, you can keep your heart open. Yes, we need to set boundaries and protect ourselves but don't protect yourself to the extent that you close your heart off from the world.

**OUR PAIN TEACHES US ABOUT TRUST**
**In difficult and painful experiences, we learn how to trust better.** For example, relationships with others can teach us to set boundaries better and understand what it takes to earn our trust first. When something does not go our way, it teaches us to trust life that what will be will be. When we ignore that gut feeling that we all have and then something doesn't go our way, we learn that we will not do that again. When people go through near-death

experiences, they often tend to say a prayer because they feel out of control, and it feels like the only thing left to do.

**Trust is everywhere, and it never leaves you. Trust is our natural way of being like breathing, but we just make it overly complicated.**

The more you trust, the freer and fulfilled you will be, and that is what I want for you, my dear reader.

### TRUSTING SOMETHING HIGHER
I want to briefly discuss the third realm of trust, the trust in something higher. This is where your faith, religion, spirituality, or whatever belief system you may have, comes in.

**One of my major beliefs is that everyone needs to believe in something.**

For some, it is God, The Universe, yourself, love, artificial intelligence, the power of nature, law of attraction; everything happens for a reason - entities of faith are endless.

You have the right to find your own faith and belief system, but you must know what you believe in because when life throws its curveballs and challenges, your faith and beliefs keep you going.

For me, it was my "everything happens for a reason" in 2017 that got me through. Then it evolved that I started to believe that there is a spiritual entity that guides me.

**Do your best, and the Universe does the rest.**
**Let go and let God.**

Trust and surrender are all over the two phrases that define my faith today. Surrender is still the part where I am spiritually growing, but the more trust I embody in myself, others, and life, the more surrender I can practice and the more I can let go and let God.

I love this phrase in Christian terms, or as sung in the famous Carrie Underwood song: *"Jesus, take the wheel."*

An excellent example of this is when I had graduated from college and was staying at a friend's house while I was figuring out my next step. My friend was very generous, allowing me to stay there for a month, and then told me they would need me to leave within three weeks. This created urgency and panic in me as I had no idea what I was going to do next.

My theater teacher, who also was a devoted Buddhist and a great source of comfort and spiritual guidance for me at the time, gave me the best advice: *"If you are panicking about this, the Universe is busy taking care of you and* won't have the time and space to actually take care of this thing you are panicking about. Calm down. Focus on something else, and it will be sorted."

My reply to that was: "CALM DOWN?!?!? Are you telling me to calm DOWN? How on earth am I supposed to CALM DOWN?"

Somehow though, I did. I let it go and focused on applying for jobs instead, and then the "Go to LA," whisper that I shared at the beginning of this book happened a week later.

**When you have done all you can and you let go and let God - the solutions will appear.** By letting go and surrendering, you make room for the answers to come in and directions to clarify.

I have often had discussions with my clients where they are stressed about deciding when there is a strict timeline. I give them that same guidance, and every time they come back telling me that solution had come after all when they had flipped their focus elsewhere and calmed themselves down.

**Trust is simple. We just complicate it.**

**When you let go and take care of yourself, you start feeling better, and the answers will come.** Everything we have covered in this book thus far has been about taking care of yourself: your health, healing, energy, your authentic being and boosting your resilience to face challenges and changes of life.

Because when you align your health, energy and are connected and learning to love and live as your authentic self, you can trust yourself and things will start falling into place. Honestly, it has happened so many times with my clients that we just do this connection work together on the self and things just start falling into place like magic.

I have had clients who needed to heal from a breakup and they wanted to heal and be ready to receive the new love they deserve, but honestly all they had to do was just to focus on the relationship themselves and love would start to present itself in their life in various ways - most importantly the love coming from within. We will talk about this in the final chapter.

**To summarize:**
**Connection to yourself changes your connection to others and beyond.**
**It is like a miracle.**
**So, dear soul. Take care of yourself.**

**Put these teachings from this book into action to connect with yourself.**

Connect with your beliefs and your relationship with trust and see where healing is needed to be able to trust more. Doing the practices from previous chapters will support your connection to trust.

Then, you can trust yourself, others, this life, and that something higher even more. You can surrender more and the answers and clarity you are after will come. Then, all you have to do is just to listen to your heart and trust it - your heart will never guide you wrong.

Your heart is the compass to living a heartful life, and we shall discuss the core essence of it next, which is *fulfillment.*

# CHAPTER SIX
# F for Fulfillment

*"Every living organism is fulfilled when it follows the right path for its own nature."*
**— Marcus Aurelius, Meditations**

What do you want? Why do you want it? What fulfills you? What does not? What is working? What is not? What do you want more of? What about less?

These are some of the most important questions I ask with my coaching clients and myself frequently.

People often speak about how they want to be happy and often seek happiness as a goal. However, as much as happiness is an excellent thing to focus on, **happiness is momentary.**

**Fulfillment is long-lasting.**

Fulfillment is what we must all strive for. To find what fills your heart is where you also find more health, healing, enthusiasm, authenticity, resilience, and trust in your life. When you do what fulfills you, your energy changes, you feel like you are authentically yourself, you feel enthusiasm regularly in your life and you also feel different in your body, too. It is all interconnected.

All this leads you to be able to trust yourself and your life more simply because you just feel *so good*.

**Everyone in this world deserves to feel fulfilled.**

Don't get me wrong, I want you to have happy moments too, but having a life where you feel fulfillment on a regular basis is where your life changes.

So, my dear reader, I have a few questions for you:

*What fills your heart in this life?*
*What gives you that feeling in your chest that it could expand from joy?*
*What gives you a powerful sense of goodness or almost a high when you experience it?*

Everyone deserves an extraordinary life that fulfills you. *You* deserve that, and it all starts with powerful questions like this.

Coach, Speaker and Accomplished Entrepreneur Ed Mylett writes in his book "#Maxout your life: Strategies for becoming an elite performer":

*"Remember, the quality of your life is equal to the quality of questions you ask yourself."*

The point Mylett makes is that your life is determined by what kind of questions you ask yourself. Your life gets as good depending on how good your questions are, and most importantly, how you answer them.

That is why coaching is powerful because it is based on the power of great questions and reflection on answers, listening and mirroring those answers so a person can raise their awareness of themselves.

I am aware that for some of you seeing the questions above regarding fulfillment might bring up an "I don't know." That is okay. That is why you are here reading this book so you can start finding answers and for you to take these questions into your journal, coaching, therapy or personal conversation space where you can explore them further to find your answers.

As just said, it all starts with questions. Coming from a journalism background where telling stories was all about asking the right questions in interviews to doing coaching and mentoring and now writing this book which is filled with journaling questions - questions are at the heart of everything I do. I believe questions are at the heart of creating your best possible life. As Mylett wrote, the better questions we ask, the better life will be. Because when we dare to do self-inquiry through powerful, sometimes very challenging, honest and even painful questions - our lives will change.

I have a simple connecting exercise to get you started.

**CONNECTING EXERCISE: DO WHAT YOU ENJOYED DOING AS A CHILD**

*What did you enjoy doing as a child?*
*When was the last time you did it?*
*Then, go do it.*

If you don't remember what you enjoyed as a child, ask someone. Find out what it was that you were fascinated by as a child. For some, it might be playing an instrument or singing. Perhaps you enjoyed horseback riding, playing football, or another sport? Maybe you loved art, putting legos together, or coloring?

It can be anything - just find out what you were drawn to as a child and then do it. Yes, even if it is coloring or putting legos together - order some legos or a coloring book online and then do it.

Trust me on this.

I mean it. **As children, we tap into our fulfillment naturally.** I tend to say children are the most heartful beings of us all because as children we are just ourselves and we feel enthusiasm and also find fulfillment naturally in our being. It is just a natural state.

As we grow up, we can lose our connection to this childlike wonder and fulfillment as we start to think about what others think and take in other external noise that gets in the way for us to be fulfilled. In addition, we might not prioritize what simply brings us joy because life with all its responsibilities and adult matters take so much space.

**This must change, my dear reader. This must change because when we make room for what fulfills us that changes the entire caliber of your being and your life.**

So, when you have found out what you enjoyed doing as a child, schedule a time for you to do it and observe how you feel and start to see the energetic shifts that start occurring and tune into your body:

*How do I feel in my body when I do the activity?*
*How is my mind feeling?*
*What is the sensation in my heart space?*
*What are the feelings most present for me during this activity?*

So, if you do not know what fulfills your heart - going back to what you enjoyed as a child can often give you an answer you seek and you might reconnect with an old hobby or activity you enjoyed doing when you were younger.

When you do what fulfills your heart, your life will start fulfilling you with more of what makes you feel good. This is so simple but works like magic. It is the same magic as gratitude. When we appreciate what we have and count our blessings, we get more things to appreciate in our lives.

**FULFILLMENT AND FLOW**

Another easy way to find out what gives you fulfillment is when you experience a sense of flow. Flow is a positive psychology concept that Mihaly Csikszentmihalyi wrote about in his book "Flow: The Psychology of Optimal Experience" in which he describes flow as a state *"in which people are so involved in an activity that nothing else seems to matter; the experience itself is so enjoyable that people will do it even at great cost, for the sheer sake of doing it."*

*When was the last time you just did something for the sake of it and were fully immersed in it that you lost track of time?*

*When was the last time you got so immersed that you forgot the basic needs like eating and going to the bathroom because you were just having such a good time and in such deep flow with something?*

**That is fulfillment in your world. That is what you must include more in your life.**

Our lives are too filled with doing things FOR something or for us to achieve or get somewhere, when in fact, that true fulfillment of life lies in doing things just for the sake of them.

Ever since I have been a kid, I have loved singing. I always sang when my mom was taking me around in a stroller as a child. I did not stop and have not stopped. To this day, I sing almost every day, whether it is while working or in a shower, or cooking. I do it just for the sake of doing it because I love it.

Only in 2022, when I was 29, I pursued singing lessons and got the courage to sing onstage. Even though it was a courageous act to follow my heart to sing onstage, and it had been an aspiration of mine all my life. At the end of the day, it was just about the singing, whether it is in a shower or onstage. I just sing because it makes me feel so free. I fully immerse myself in it and lose track of time.

So, as you can see, my fulfillment comes from something I loved doing even as a child, and it is also something where I experience a sense of flow.

You have that within you too. Everyone has something - we just gotta connect with it. All you have to do is ask the questions and find the answers from within you. They are there - you might have just forgotten.

**FULFILLMENT AND MEANING**

*"He, who has a why to live for, can bear with almost any how."*

**— Victor Frankl**

I have to briefly touch on another element within fulfillment: meaning.

I touched on meaning also in Chapter Four on resilience and how the adversity and pain we go through can really be turned into power by finding meaning in it all and using it as fuel to drive a purpose.

When we have a strong why to do what we do. When the why is strong, there is a deep meaning rooted so deep within our being that nobody can take it away.

**When there is deep meaning, there will also be fulfillment.**

To give you an example, every time I hold my "More Espresso, Less Depresso" women's meetups in London where we bring our hearts into a safe, confidential space where we can openly share what is going on in our lives and get support from each other - all done over a cup of coffee or tea. Every time I have held that space, I feel so fulfilled from the feeling of having done something meaningful.

*My why is to help people keep connecting and moving through life's ups and downs to see that there is always light at the end of the tunnel - no matter how dark the tunnel might seem at the time.*

Sometimes all it takes is just a cup of coffee and connecting with a group of women who all felt called to be there to find healing, connection, and strength in togetherness. Seeing how the women leave the space feeling lighter every time is everything to me. All it takes is community, shared experiences, and connection to see the light at the end of the tunnel - and that is the ethos that my Connected You Community stands on.

My why is helping people to see the light at the end of the tunnel no matter how dark it seems. My why is my brother, who we lost way too soon because he was in a dark tunnel and could not find his way back to the light. This is why I live for. This is my why I do everything I do.

When we take meaningful action from our why - fulfillment follows.

**So, when you find your why - act from it, and even more fulfillment will be embodied.**

**So, how can you find your why?**

Again, it starts with two of the most powerful questions you can ask yourself:

*Who are you?*
*And why do you do what you do?*

This also links to our beliefs which we covered in Chapter Five.

**What you believe in links to who you are and why you do what you do.**

I have given you many journal prompts in this book, but these are among the most powerful and biggest questions of all. These are questions that, once explored with yourself, I encourage to bring into a coaching space to elevate it and deepen your connection to them.

**The answers to these questions really bring out the explanation of who you truly are and why you are here. When you have those answers covered - everything falls**

**into place. Every other element we have covered in this book falls into place, and heartfulness settles in.**

As a side note, as I have said before, all of these elements are interlinked. Heartfulness is about the interconnection of everything. I wrote about this in my thesis study, where one of the themes I concluded was that yoga teachers linked heartfulness to this sense of "oneness" and being part of something greater. We are all interconnected, and so is everything in this method.

How I use this method as a coach is intuitive. HEARTFUL does not happen in a linear order, but the themes of HEARTFUL are covered in the order that feels right to the person I am connecting with and coaching. Sometimes, we start with this element of Fulfillment - the flow, the who, and the why; for others, it might be another element where we begin.

**I believe to give the most powerful coaching, you meet the person where they are at and adapt your method for them. Every human is unique because no human is the same.**

To wrap this chapter, fulfillment indeed entails and interconnects all the elements we have covered thus far in the previous chapters of this book.

When you experience fulfillment in your life, you:

- *Can find your health and physical state feeling better.*
- *Find different outlets where healing can occur.*
- *Experience enthusiasm frequently in your life.*
- *Authenticity becomes your normal. You know yourself, and you know where you are being your free true self.*
- *Boost your resilience within you to get through the ups and downs of life.*
- *You trust yourself, others, and something higher.*

Having gotten this far in this book, you are now aware of the six first elements that are key elements of heartful living. After all, awareness and understanding is the first step toward anything.

We will speak about understanding next and then cover the last element, which, even though it might be last, is the most powerful one of them all.

# CHAPTER SEVEN
## U for Understanding

*"Nothing in life is to be feared, it is only to be understood. Now is the time to understand more, so that we may fear less."*

— Marie Curie

I have a question for you: Do you understand yourself and how you tick? *Truly.*

**From the holistic understanding of your experience, you can take more courageous heart-led actions. You can cross that bridge to heartful action only from a place of understanding. Without understanding, you cannot act on anything with full intention and clarity and manifest your vision.**

I love personal development, self-help, and psychology, and I am writing this book to promote self-awareness in people, which leads to deeper understanding.

**Seeking a deep understanding of yourself, your story, what has happened for you, and your life is key to a connected heartful life.**

What you have gone through has made you who you are today and all that you are also are the ingredients for you to be your most heartful self on this earth.

You have all the answers; however, getting to those answers within can be difficult. That is why I think the most powerful vessel of self-discovery is coaching.

A coach holds space for you to find those answers within you. It is not a coach's job to tell you what to do or give you the answers, but to ask powerful questions, act as a mirror to reflect what you have laid out back to you for you to see, and hold a safe space for you to get honest with yourself and do the work.

A coach has a toolbox that can help you find those answers and, most importantly, help you take action on those answers outside the sessions. We can talk about things all day long, but if no aligned action is taken, nothing changes.

**Nothing changes if nothing changes.**

**So, you must understand yourself, so you can take actions from that connected place that can change your life to what you want it to be. The other elements of the HEARTFUL method we have covered are all part of the journey toward understanding.**

**You must understand your health** to optimize it so you can live a heartful life.

**You must understand what needs healing** so it can be given the space it needs and you can live a healthier life in connection with yourself, with others and something higher.

**Your energy is your greatest asset and understanding it is key.** The energy you give returns to you, so tapping into the highest possible energy and learning how to optimize your energy is key for making your life vision a reality.

**Understanding who you are at your authentic self** is everything because you deserve to live your own heart-led fulfilled courageous story that you know, can own and just be in freely.

**Understanding what your resilience looks like,** and how it has become critical for you to tap into it to keep moving through the ups and downs in life. Adversity is an inevitable part of life, and it is from our adversity that we actually can gain most of our understanding and empowerment, if we dare to face and feel it to free it.

**You need to understand your relationship with trust in** yourself, others, and something higher to find inner peace. Next to fulfillment - peace is the inner state we must strive for. When we have our peace, nobody and nothing can shake us because our trust is so strong.

**You need to understand what gives you inner fulfillment**, flow and meaning in your life. When you know who you are, your why and what fulfills you, it changes your life.

**The final part that we have yet to cover is the understanding of your relationship with love** and to come to terms of how conditional your love for yourself is and where those conditions have morphed.

**Heartfulness is unconditional love.** We will speak about love in this next and final chapter of this book.

Therefore, understanding is key. We need to learn to understand before we can practice, take action and embody something fully. **To become heartful is to understand and embody all of its elements.** It is a life-long practice that I have dedicated my life to and this book is my invitation for you to join me on this transformative journey.

**My hope for you, my dear reader, is that you learn to understand yourself holistically through these eight elements we cover in this book, so you can make**

**changes and take courageous action toward a life where your heart feels full.**

I hope this book has given you tools and insight to get to more of an understanding of yourself and what heartfulness is from the point of view of what I have studied and experienced in my life. Maybe you have been able to take some insights and start actioning on them already or maybe it has sparked curiosity for you to learn more or it has just given you some food for thought. Either way, if the outcome was any of those for you, I have fulfilled my intention with this book.

**All I want is for more people to understand how this lifestyle is accessible to everyone.** I have wanted to illustrate how I walk the talk of this HEARTFUL lifestyle, so you can do the same. I wanted to write this book so you can start within your own remit independently and take it to any coaching or therapy space to continue. Of course, if you feel called to reach out to me to do 1:1 work or join any of my group sessions, I would love to have you join my heartful Connected You tribe - which is all about us living heartfully and connecting within, with each other and something higher.

If this book has served you in any way, please share this with someone from your circle to spread the message. Sharing is caring and the more people understand this, the more heartful energy we can create on this earth and the more heartful this world can be.

Doesn't that just sound exciting?

I am just a small part of this movement, but you my lovely reader are the growth of this movement as you go about your life to understand yourself and embody heartfulness in your daily life and that way inspiring the same in others.

But before we fully close this book journey, we have one more element to understand, which is *love*.

# CHAPTER EIGHT
# L for Love

*"The heart is the thousand-stringed instrument that can only be tuned with love."*
**— Hazif**

Love being the most powerful energy of all is where the HEARTFUL method ends and starts. Love is everything. As you journey toward heartfulness, love is at the end and at every stage of it all. You do not need to look for love externally because you are *it*.

Matt Kahn has a practice in his book *"Whatever arises, love that: A love revolution that begins with you"* on how to surrender to the heart by creating your own love statement that includes the words you have needed to hear externally, and at the end of the day, you just need to say them to yourself. Your brain does not know the difference between you saying them or someone else.

**We look for validation and love externally when we actually need to validate and love ourselves.**

I searched for this externally for a long time until reading Kahn's book made me realize I was looking for validation in my relationships because I had never validated myself.

Heartfulness starts from connection and love within; part of that is for you to validate yourself.

Kahn's process begins with the question:

"*What are the words that you always needed to hear from someone else? Give them to yourself.*"

This is a powerful question to meditate and journal on. If you learn to give yourself the love you deserve, especially when faced with hurt, you'll naturally love yourself more the more life challenges you. **Love yourself through it all. Love yourself through all the challenges and heartbreaks.** The ones hurting are the ones that need the love the most, and you giving it to yourself will reflect the love that person and the world needs.

Kahn writes in his book that profound healing occurs when you realize in hardships that **you are worth more love, not less, and you give yourself that.** When you connect with that love within you and it becomes a natural practice, you live from the energy of love and more love and energy of that high frequency will enter your life.

**When you honor yourself and love yourself, your intuition of the heart will start to trust you and give you guidance on how to make choices based on love**.

If someone says the loving thing is to let go cause they are not aligned and loving in themselves - that is true. **For people to align themselves in love within is a foundation for any relationships with others to flourish.**

**If you do not thrive in love within, nothing else can either. Love your inner child. Give yourself what you have always needed from someone else. Give yourself the love you need.**

As I mentioned in Chapter Four on Resilience, the painful and challenging experiences we go through actually are the pathway to our heartful selves, because **our greatest heartbreaks are just a sign how much we loved.**

**Love is everywhere. Even in the pain.**

However, through healing through this method, I hope everyone will get to a place where unconditional love is ever present.

Learning to love yourself unconditionally through whatever comes in life is freedom. The more you love yourself the more it reflects to the world, creating a more loving world. Energy radiates and the energy you show up in the world will radiate back to you. That is why the work of chapter 2 and getting your energy and enthusiasm aligned is key.

**Loving yourself is where heartfulness really begins, as it does with every other element of this method. Heartfulness always starts from the connection with *yourself*.**

So, to finish the journey in this book, I will run through some powerful points to get you started on your journey toward unconditional love.

## THE POWER OF SOLITUDE

We live in a world where we talk about love all the time and seek it, when it is within us all along. We do not need to find it. We need to just reconnect with the energy of love within us.

You cannot love others if you are not in love with yourself.

I was not in love with myself for many many years. I did not love myself unconditionally. Through this method, I have had to connect with myself in solitude and learn to love myself.

This is the best relationship advice I have ever gotten: *Be the relationship you want with yourself first.*

As I said in the beginning, give yourself the love you seek. This will change everything for you.

**People come and go, but your relationship with yourself is for life.** So, why would you seek love from someone else who might not be an embodiment of love themselves - but also seeking that from you? This is why relationships get messy and divorce rates are high.

*We need to take more time to date ourselves before we go on dates with others.*

Many of you might already be in a relationship when reading this, but this even applies to *you.*

*When was the last time you took yourself on a date?*
*When was the last time you really focused on the relationship with yourself?*
*When was the last time you gave yourself the love you needed?*

We all must keep that relationship with ourselves in check.
We must love ourselves first before anyone else because we cannot love or live from an empty cup.
We must show up with love to ourselves consistently.

In Jay Shetty's Book "8 Rules of Love: How to Find It, Keep It, and Let It Go Book" he shares this quote from the Buddha that summarizes this perfectly.

*"When you like a flower, you simply pluck it. But when you love a flower, you water it every day."*

You must water yourself, nourish yourself, love yourself - *every day.*
Self-love like everything else in this book is a practice. We must show up for ourselves and then we can give more in this world as well.

So, the next exercise I have for you is to arrange a date with yourself using the five love languages.

**THE FIVE LOVE LANGUAGES BY GARY CHAPMAN**
Words of affirmation
Quality time
Physical touch
Acts of service
Receiving gifts

These love languages are often discussed in the context of relationships with others, but I run a workshop on love languages where we focus on connecting to them and create a self-love practice you need at this time to nourish your relationship with yourself. **We all have a specific love language that we are mostly connected to - and it can change in different parts of life which love language you need to focus on.**

If you feel you do not know which love language you are most connected to at this time, you can go on 5 Love Languages website to find out your love language through a quiz. You can find the link in the references page at the end of this book.

I'll explain the context of each love language and what that could look like for you briefly through these questions for connection:

*What do you feel you need most at this time to feel a bit more wholesome within yourself?*

Words of affirmation
Quality time
Physical touch
Acts of service
Receiving gifts

*If you had that partner, or if you do have one, what would you need from them right now the most with the specific love language you chose?*

Then give that to yourself. Here are some ideas for you.

*Do you need words of affirmation? Go journal on the beautiful question I shared in the beginning of this* chapter from Matt Kahn. "*What are the words that you always needed to hear from someone else? Give them to yourself.*"

**Needing quality time?** *Well, if you took yourself on your dream date - what would that look like for you? Then go for it.*

**Do you need physical touch?** *Go get a massage, hot bath or perhaps you need to masturbate and have time for pleasure.*

**Do you wish someone did an act of service for you?** *Clean your entire apartment and closets to declutter and clear energy.*

**Or, maybe you want to buy yourself a nice gift?** *Buy yourself the flowers you wish your partner bought for you or the one gift you hope they would get you for Christmas.*

**Give yourself the love you wish someone else had.**
**Connect with yourself. Love yourself.**
**Date yourself. Be the relationship you desire with yourself first.**
Loving you this way will change the course of all your external relationships as well - both romantic and platonic. Trust me. When you start with connection to self, the connection to others and something higher shifts, too.

## THE POWER OF FORGIVENESS

The final part that I want to touch on in this book is forgiveness.

Forgiveness is one of the most powerful forms of love.

When mistreated by someone, it is easy to want to just mistreat them back. However, **remembering that "hurt people hurt people" and hurt people need the most love of all is important. Showing love for yourself is actually a mirror of love that radiates and heals the people around you with the love you give to yourself.**

Even if a loving action is for you to take yourself out of a specific situation and wish them best, the love will radiate all the same.

**It takes a lot of heart to be able to embody love to such an extent that you are able to love even when the person might have caused you the greatest pain. Sometimes, the only form of love we can work toward in those situations is forgiveness.**

**You must forgive those who hurt you greatest, my dear reader.** Only then you can truly free yourself from what can feel like the chains of your past and be free in the now with your whole self.

**Also, you might not be able to show love and kindness to the person, but for you to love yourself and being kind to yourself is what will beat the hate.** Hate upon hate only will cause more of that energy, but love on hate beats it because the energy of love is much more powerful.

I mentioned earlier in this book my journey of EMDR therapy and that really helped to find forgiveness to those who have hurt me and free myself from the anger and pain I carried. I cannot highlight enough about the power of therapy. There are so many forms out there for you to find what is best for you to find your own path to healing. I would not be here if it weren't for the therapy and coaching I have done in these past few years.

When we forgive, we set ourselves free and these final exercises of this book will set you on a beautiful way to get started because even if this book ends, your journey starts and what better way to start than forgiveness?

## HO'OPONOPONO PRAYER OF FORGIVENESS

This is a Hawaiian forgiveness ritual and prayer that you can practice at the comfort of your home is one of the most profounding practices of forgiveness I know - and you can do it at home for free.

It connects us back to love and is a simple medicine and healing through the power of meditation. It can be that first step of making things right whoever you might not be on the best terms with at this time - to apologize, ask for forgiveness, embody gratitude and love.

*"In common with other shamanic traditions, the Hawaiian tradition teaches that all life is connected. Ho'oponopono is, therefore, not only a way of healing ourselves, but others and our world as well."*

**— Timothy Freke, Shamanic Wisdomkeepers**

**It goes like this:**
*I am sorry.*
*(Please) Forgive me.*
*Thank you.*
*I love you.*

There are various recordings of this online that can help you get started where they will repeat these four phrases and you can meditate on them. There might be a specific person that comes to you as you read this that you feel this kind of practice is needed - or sometimes if you just step into this ritual - and it might reveal you a person who you need to have this connecting moment with.

## CONNECTING EXERCISE: FORGIVENESS LETTER

*Who in your life or from your past you want to and need to forgive to find more freedom within yourself?* You might already have someone in mind or even have quite a few. List their names out who you wish to forgive to find more inner freedom and peace.

Then, one by one, write a letter to each of them. Say everything you want to say to them. And I mean everything. If you are angry at them, say it. Just say everything to them first but then conclude the letter by saying how you are ready to forgive them. How you desire to set yourself free from the weight you are carrying and just wish them well. Sometimes a part of a journey might be even to write it even if there might be some resistance.

It is like saying "I love you" to the mirror to yourself. It might feel so uncomfortable to say such a thing out loud to yourself and maybe you don't fully believe in it as you say it - but if you keep saying it daily, the more you start believing it. The same thing applies with forgiveness - there might be resistance in saying the Ho'oponopono or writing letters of forgiveness but if you allow yourself to move through the resistance - keep saying it and writing anyway what comes - it will set you free.

Say what you gotta say. Feel what you gotta feel to free it.

Words are power. That is why I believe in the power of journaling, and this book has a lot of journaling exercises because the power of questions and answers are the way to find understanding - which was the seventh element of this book.

I always think Nelson Mandela is one of the most heartful forgiving people to have set foot on this Earth to set as an example when it comes to love and forgiveness. I will end this chapter on his remarkable words that summarize the lesson here.

*"People must learn to hate, and if they can learn to hate, they can be taught to love, for love comes more naturally to the human heart than its opposite."*
**— Nelson Mandela**

We go through dark tunnels in this life, but we can always find the light at the end of it. Like electricity, we can disconnect at times but we can find our way back to connection to love and light again.

Love and light is our most natural being. We embody that naturally as children but can lose sight of it as we face challenges and pain in life.

We must relearn and recondition ourselves back to love, and I hope this book and these eight elements of the HEARTFUL method can help you in that journey.

**HEARTFUL is a journey not for the faint-hearted but one where wholeheartedness and freedom resides, if you find the courage within you to go on that journey.**

You being here reading this book tells me that you have it within you. You have already started - and even though this might be the end of this book.

It is only the beginning for you.

# EPILOGUE

Wow. We did it. We made it to the end of this book journey.

I cannot believe it.

I hope this book has given you some powerful tools and a place to begin. A starting place for you to connect with yourself, others and something higher through the elements of this HEARTFUL method for you to at least understand what this entails and start making changes toward a more heartful life for yourself.

**To give yourself the gift of heartful living is the greatest gift of all.**

**I dream of a heartful world where people are holistically connected with their mind, heart, body and soul and are intuitively awake to courageously pursue a life that feels like theirs** and where they feel fulfilled. Where enthusiasm is experienced frequently and love is the energy we live from for the highest good for all.

I dream of a world where people's suffering is met with love and kindness and you can feel you are not alone. How actually you can be healed by seeing that your heartbreak is not there to break you down but to break you open. How, eventually, you can break free to become who you truly are at your essence. You are that already, you might have just forgotten how to be.

**I hope you get not only the life you want, but you get the life you deserve, my dear reader.**

I dream of a world where love wins and more heartful energy is felt in this world, **as the more heartful the world, the more light there will be.** The more heartful the world, the more people can see there is always light at the end of the tunnel - no matter how dark the tunnel might seem for them at the time.

This book would have not come to be if I did not pursue the courageous journey of my heart from moving to the US, taking the leap to go to LA, study positive psychology and pursue EMDR and all these other healing journeys in the past few years.

**The fact you read this book shows me you have the courage within, too.** Thank you for being here and know if there is anything I can do to support you on your journey, you have a guide in me ready to embark on this journey by your side whether it is in person or from afar. I am rooting for you.

**And just know this: You have everything within you to do this.**

I hope I've managed to hold space for you through this book for your own self-inquiry on what HEARTFUL means to you, and that is what I will leave you with.

**One more question which is the end of this book journey but the beginning of your chapter as you embark on your own journey of heartful living outside these pages.**

## *What does the word HEARTFUL mean to you?*

As with every word we live by, we must define it for ourselves. And from that meaning, **enjoy your journey of what I hope will be a life-long courageous adventure of heartfulness - whatever that may look like for you.**

Keep connecting and keep moving through it all, you beautiful soul.

We are in this together - to move through the roller-coaster of heartbreaks and heartful moments, and everything in between, that makes life such a beautiful, wonderful ride.

From my heart to yours,

Essi xx

# RESOURCES

Throughout this book, I refer to my thesis study *"Heartfulness is connection": Yoga teachers' understanding and experience of heartfulness."* You can download it for free from my shop on my website at essiaugustevirtanen.co.

**Prologue**

Murphy-Shigematsu, M. (2018). *From Mindfulness to Heartfulness: Transforming Self and Society with Compassion.* Berrett-Koehler Publishers, Inc.

**H for Health and Healing**

Suggested experts for gut health to support you on your journey:

Nutrition Scientist and Professor Tim Spector
With over 1,000 original articles published in some of the world's top scientific journals makes him in the top 1% most cited scientists on the planet. https://tim-spector.co.uk/

Dr. Vincent Pedre also known as the American Gut Doctor
happygutlife.com

**E for Energy and Enthusiasm**

Cambridge Dictionary web source:
https://dictionary.cambridge.org/dictionary/english/enthusiasm

Dale, C. (2020). *Llewellyn's little book of chakras.*
Woodbury, MN, US. Llewellyn Publications.

Pert, C. (1997). *Molecules of emotion.* New York, NY, US.
Touchstone.

Maslow, A. H. (1971). *The farther reaches of human nature.*
New York, NY, US: Arkana/Penguin Books.

"Energy Check-In" questionnaire copyright by Essi
Auguste Virtanen

**A for Authenticity**

Murphy-Shigematsu, M. (2018). *From Mindfulness to
Heartfulness: Transforming Self and Society with
Compassion.* Berrett-Koehler Publishers, Inc.

Smith, J. A., & Osborn, M. (2015). *Interpretative
phenomenological analysis as a useful methodology for
research on the lived experience of pain.* British journal of
pain, 9(1), 41–42. https://doi.org/10.1177/2049463714541642

Joseph, S. (2019). *Authentic: How to be yourself and why it
matters.* Piatkus.

Authenticity formula by Stephen Joseph:
http://www.authenticityformula.com/

What is EMDR? | Types of therapy. (n.d.).
https://www.bacp.co.uk/about-therapy/types-of-
therapy/eye-movement-desensitisation-and-reprocessing-
emdr/

Values in Action questionnaire online:

https://www.viacharacter.org/

Linley, A. (2008). *Average to A+: Realising strengths in yourself and others.* CAPP Press.

**R for Resilience**

Marie Stejskal, T. (2023). *The 5 Practices of Highly Resilient People: Why Some Flourish When Others Fold.* Hachette Co.

Pemberton, C. (2015). *Resilience: A practical guide for coaches.* Open University Press.

Boniwell, I., & Tunariu, A. D. (2019). *Positive psychology: Theory, research and applications.* Open University Press.

Neenan, M. (2018). *Developing resilience: A cognitive-behavioural approach.* Routledge.

Miralles, F. & García, H. (2020). *The Book of Ichigo Ichie: The Art of Making the Most of Every Moment, the Japanese Way.* Quercus.

Murphy-Shigematsu, M. (2018). *From Mindfulness to Heartfulness: Transforming Self and Society with Compassion.* Berrett-Koehler Publishers, Inc.

The Five Stages of Grief created by Elisabeth Kübler-Ross and David Kesslerhttps://grief.com/the-five-stages-of-grief/

Kessler, D. (2020). *Finding Meaning: The Sixth Stage of Grief.* Simon and Schuster, Scribner imprint.

Grief.com - Sixth Stage of Grief: https://grief.com/sixth-stage-of-grief/

**T for Trust**
Vanzant, I. (2017). *Trust: Mastering the Four Essential Trusts: Trust in Self, Trust in God, Trust in Others, Trust in Life.* Smiley Books.

**F for Fulfillment**
Mylett, E. (2018). *#Maxout your life: Strategies for becoming an elite performer.* Mylett Communications.

Csikszentmihalyi, M. (2008). *Flow: The Psychology of Optimal Experience.* Ingram International Inc.

**U for Understanding**

Frankl, V. E. (2004). *Man's Search for Meaning: The classic tribute to hope from the Holocaust.* Rider.

**L for Love**

Kahn, M. (2016). *Whatever arises, love that: A love revolution that begins with you.* Sounds True.

Shetty, J. (2023). *8 rules of love: How to find it, keep it, and let it go.* Thorsons.

Chapman, G. (2015) *The 5 love languages: The secret to love that lasts.* Moody Publishers.

Five Love Languages Quiz online:
https://5lovelanguages.com/quizzes/love-language

# HEARTFUL STORIES

I wanted to take a moment to give space for some amazing client stories who I have had the pleasure to work with along the years. Besides me walking the talk, it is their stories that make this method real. These stories inspire me to this day and show me how this heartful living is possible not just for me, but for others, too.

*"Essi taught me the value of connection, something I hadn't recognised before. She helped me understand the connection that exists between my heart and mind and how this can be used to better yourself. I learnt how to connect with my heart, mind and body in everyday life which seriously improved my mood and mental state."*

— **Mayowa Fehintola, London, UK**

*"Essi reminded me the importance of following your heart and the journey from the mind to heart is a beautiful one filled with boundless energy and heart filled connections."*

— **Kathy Drummond, London, UK**

*"Essi's 'coaching way of being' as a unique, humanistic, transparent, safe and encouraging, has helped me to understand myself more fully; I have been able to connect with my authentic self better instead of the idealist view that I have had about myself."*

— **Sandra Suomela, London, UK**

*"Essi's coaching undoubtedly changed my life for the better. I felt overwhelmed by the future, unsure of which path to take and where my next step should be. Essi guided me through my own self-exploration; finding a clear direction and alleviating an insurmountable number of stresses that were hindering me from moving forward. Through these sessions with Essi, I have found inner peace, rekindled relationships and have found a new*

*meaning to my life. I am forever grateful and excited for the future ahead!"*

**— Brianna Howard, Missouri, USA**

*"With a positive attitude and by asking the right questions, Essi pushed me to discover deeper into my soul and find the answers inside of me that I had had all along, but just couldn't find without the help. In summary, Essi helped me to find my direction, my purpose and I will be forever grateful. From now on, I will do everything to make my dreams come true. I could call Essi a life saver."*

**— Laura Kolari, Tahko, Finland**

*"Despite what others might see from the outside, I truly felt lost, isolated and a tad bit scared of opening up to my present. I was holding on to my past for dear life, and lived with a sense of rejection towards my surroundings. Through her guidance, Essi helped me weave my own way out of that darker place and made me realize there was an entire dimension of things I was missing out on."*

**— Daniela Davila, Cali, Colombia**

*"Essi has the instinctively organic ability to completely empathise with whatever you're going through, connect the dots and ask the right questions at the right time. She allows the space to just be present and reflect. The activities she gave me, or did with me in our sessions, were uncomfortable but completely perfect for how I was feeling that week."*

**— Eleanor Russell, Epsom, UK**

I hope you are inspired by these brave people who took the step toward a more heartful life and to show you how you can do the same.

# ABOUT THE AUTHOR

## Essi Auguste Virtanen

Essi Auguste Virtanen is an intuitive coach, mentor, writer and community builder based in London supporting individuals to connect with themselves after heartbreaking experiences in their lives to turn their pain into their authentic power and heartful purpose. Essi hopes to support individuals to find their own version of HEARTFUL living. Essi does both 1:1 work and also does group sessions and events through her community Connected You.

With an innate ability to bring people together, Essi, drawing from her background in journalism, understands the power of shared narratives in healing and uniting us. Guided by coaching principles and positive psychology,

Essi established Connected You Community first as a sanctuary for women, but now hoping this community to be a space for humanity to come together from all polarities as a whole to navigate life's uncertainties, with the resounding belief that together is better. Amidst the collective journey, answers can be uncovered and paths illuminated.

She believes connection is the foundation for optimized mental health and holistic wellbeing to end the epidemic of loneliness, depression and separation in this world.

Connect with me:
Email: hello@connectedyou.co
Website: essiaugustevirtanen.co
Instagram: @essiauguste
LinkedIn: essiavirtanen

# JOIN MY COMMUNITY. LET'S CONNECT.

To be the first to know about upcoming events and receive exclusive content, please join our mailing list by scanning the code below or go to our website: connectedyou.co.

## I WOULD LOVE TO HEAR FROM YOU.

Please tag me in your photos on social media about this book. I would love to follow your journey of heartful living. I would love to hear what is your favorite element of the method that serves you the most - please DM me on Instagram at @essiauguste and tag me in your photos using the hashtag #IamHEARTFUL

Let's start this HEARTFUL movement together.
Thank you for being here.

Printed in Great Britain
by Amazon

36877777R00086